CLICK
POWER

Drive More Traffic, Leads, and Sales

MEREDITH OLIVER, MIRM, MCSP

For more information or bulk orders, please email meredith@creatingwow.com or call 866-227-9769.

www.CreatingWOW.com

ISBN 978-0-9848684-8-3

Also by Meredith Oliver

The Fan Factor
25 Slam Dunk Secrets to Engage Customers, Increase Referrals and Boost Sales

Table of Contents

Book Meredith Oliver to Speak at Your Next Event

Connect With Meredith

The Fan Factor: 25 Slam Dunk Secrets to Engage Customers, Increase Referrals and Boost Sales

End Notes

ABOUT THE AUTHOR

Meredith Oliver, aka The Digital Diva, helps home builders drive more traffic, leads, and sales. She is a professional speaker, consultant, and founder of Creating WOW, a digital marketing and sales training company located in Raleigh, NC.

Meredith holds a Master's Degree in Communication Technology from the prestigious Rollins College and a Bachelor of Arts Degree, majoring in Psychology, from the University of Central Florida. During the dot-com boom and bust, she worked for Move.com (now Builders Digital Experience, theBDX.com) as Regional Sales Manager. Meredith has both the education and the real world experience to help you WOW your customers online and offline.

Meredith has been speaking professionally for fifteen years. She is a thirteen-time presenter at the National Association of Home Builders International Builders Show. She is a frequent speaker and moderator of the National Sales and Marketing Council's Super Sales Rally and Sales Management Summit. Her convention seminars are consistently standing room only and rated by attendees among the most popular, entertaining, and educational seminars offered. Meredith speaks at a number of local and regional home builder association events like 21 Century Building Expo and Conference and the Southeast Builders Conference and Expo.

Meredith is one of three speakers in the Three Elements Rally, which appears to sold-out audiences internationally. She is a member of the National Association of Home Builders (NAHB), Immediate Past Chair of the Institute of Residential Marketing (MIRM), and an approved instructor for IRM and CSP courses. She holds the Master Certified New

Home Sales Professional (MCSP) designation and served as a local Sales and Marketing Council Chair and the Florida Sales & Marketing Council Chair. She is currently the Chair of the Professional Women in Building Communications Committee and the incoming President of the Carolinas National Speakers Association.

Creating WOW delivers digital marketing solutions to homebuilders, including website design, search engine optimization, paid search marketing management, and social media management

Meredith is also the author of two books, *Click Power: Drive More Traffic, Leads, and Sales* and *The Fan Factor: 25 Slam Dunk Secrets to Engage Customers, Increase Referrals and Boost Sales.*

Meredith currently lives in Raleigh, NC with her husband, son, and two shih tzus.

ACKNOWLEDGEMENTS

The picture above my desk reads: *Inspiration—many people have gone further than they imagined they could because somebody else thought they could.* How true. I couldn't have made it as far as I have without all the support and encouragement of the people around me.

- **For my number one fan**, best friend, and love of my life, Allen Oliver. Creating WOW Communications, my Master's degree, our family, and this book would not exist without you. You make me a better person every day we spend together.

- **For Brady Allen Oliver,** who is (by far) my best WOW yet.

- **For my parents and brother**, Rodney, Carla, and Parker Miller, who taught me it is okay to be an independent, smart business woman who can do anything she wants to do.

- **For Melinda Brody, John Palumbo, and Kerry Mulcrone** who are the best coaches, cheerleaders, and confidants a girl could have.

- **For the team members at Creating WOW,** who make sure our business runs smoothly despite my hectic travel schedule.

I thank all of you for your contribution to my journey.

CHAPTER 1

Why Ask Why?

WHEN WE MOVED from Florida to North Carolina, I researched, planned, and executed every aspect of the move online—everything from finding a place to live to selecting a pediatrician. Google made the moving process so much easier. We didn't make multiple visits to the area before the move or wait until after we moved to drive around and look for services. Instead, I viewed our options, narrowed down the list, and scheduled appointments all from my computer and mobile phone.

What was the last product or service you bought online? According to a 2013 GE Capital Retail Bank's second annual Major Purchase Shopper Study, 81 percent of consumers go online before they go to a store. This statistic is up 20 percent from 2012. They spend an average of seventy-nine days researching information, 60 percent start by visiting a search engine, and 88 percent made their final purchase in-store.[1] We know this as consumers, but why as business owners are we hesitant, skeptical, and in denial about the power of online marketing for our business?

When I use the term online marketing, I refer to the process of marketing your homes online. **It is critical to understand that having a website is not the same as online marketing.** Think of your website like a business card. If you keep all of your business cards in your purse, wallet, or desk drawer, sales will not increase. The act of handing your business card to a prospective customer and conversing about your product or service is active marketing, which will increase your sales.

The same holds true for your website. Online marketing is the process of pulling visitors into your website through search engines, mobile advertising, email marketing, and social media networks like Facebook and Twitter.

Ask yourself the following questions:

- How will prospective customers find my website if they don't know my business name or website address?

- More importantly, how is that lack of awareness holding my business back in terms of leads and sales?

- What could my business achieve with a broader audience?

- Am I willing to spend time and money to find out?

When I first started Creating WOW more than twelve years ago, it was the early days of the Internet and my job was to convince home builders they needed to shift from print advertising to online marketing. It was a tough sale. Most builders at that time were completely reliant on print advertising and not open to the digital world.

Through the years, most home builders have adopted digital marketing as a necessity. Today, I spend less time talking about **why** Web marketing is important and more time teaching home builders **how** to market effectively online.

However, on occasion, I still have the "why" conversation. If you are unconvinced about the power of online marketing, here are ten serious reasons why you need Web marketing to grow your sales. Hopefully, this will convince you to make a commitment to the digital world.

1. Location, location, location. In the physical world, location is everything. The importance of location is a time-tested fact that no one would argue. It's no different in the virtual world. Your customers are online researching and shopping for products to buy. According to a 2014 Pew Internet survey about the demographics of Internet users,[2] 87 percent of men and women (respectively) use the Internet daily. It's not just young people online either. More than 90 percent of men and women ages thirty through forty-nine are online and 88 percent in the fifty to sixty-four age range. In households with an income of $50,000 – $74,000, 93 percent are online and 97 percent of college graduates. Sounds like ideal customers. Think of the Web like the greatest shopping mall ever built. If you owned a retail store wouldn't you want to open a shop in the most popular, highly trafficked mall in town? You can. Your website acts as your storefront in the mall. Your customers are already online using search engines to research products and services to buy every day.

2. **Broaden your reach.** If the overwhelming majority of people research or purchase products and services online, then by marketing online you have the opportunity to reach more people. Right now you are restricted to people who drive by your neighborhood sign, view your newspaper or magazine ad, hear your radio commercial, or meet you in person. The beauty of the digital world lies in the availability to reach buyers around the world 24/7/365 on a small marketing budget. Potential customers may not have heard your name before, but with one Google search they are quickly directed to the front door of your virtual store. They can also *email* your website to a friend, *like* you on Facebook, or *tweet* about you on Twitter. This is word-of-mouth marketing on steroids.

3. **Measure and refine.** The magic of Web marketing lies in the metrics. Everything from the number of website visits to content viewed is trackable. Tracking user habits allows a company to try new marketing ideas, measure conversion results, and refine marketing tactics. No other marketing tactic allows for such precise tracking and measurement. In future chapters I will dive into website analytics and teach you the most important metrics to track. All you need to know right now is that if it's *clickable*, it's *trackable* and that makes Web marketing the best return on investment of all marketing tactics.

4. Target and qualify. Since Web marketing has advanced tracking abilities, it is easy to spend your marketing dollars wisely. For example, with Facebook ads, you can specify the age range, location, and gender of consumers you want to view your online ads and then track the traffic flow to your website. Essentially, you can run an online campaign specifically targeted to the zip codes you serve, with enough household income to afford your product. Genius. More targeted online marketing results in higher quality traffic to your website, which will result in a higher conversion rate of sales both online and offline. Since everything online is trackable, you will know exactly how well the campaign works.

5. Reduce your marketing budget. Yes, you have to spend money on digital marketing to make money. This adage is true about any facet of your business. You have to invest in inventory to have something to sell. You have to pay overhead costs like rent and wages. All of these costs are things you have to do to sell your homes. Think of marketing like one more required line item. If you don't market the inventory you've invested in, how will you sell it? The good news is that Web marketing is far more cost-effective than any other form of marketing. It will also save you a lot of money and produce a greater return on investment.

6. Women are online big time. Women are one of the most overlooked consumer target markets, yet we know women are the primary influencer in the home-buying process. Women directly account for, or influence, 85 percent of purchase decisions today, according to She-cono-my.com.[3] This website also found that women account for:

- 91 percent of new homes
- 80 percent of health care
- 93 percent of food
- 65 percent of new cars
- 93 percent of over-the-counter medications

Women are a powerful purchasing group, and the most effective way to reach them is online. The report from comScore.com on online usage titled, *Women on the Web: How Women are Shaping the Internet*,[4] provides an in-depth analysis of the online female user. "In the U.S., women are more avid online buyers than men, with 12.5 percent of female Internet users making an online purchase in February 2010, compared with nearly 10 percent of men." The report also found that women are looking to save time and money, and spend 20 percent more time on retail websites than men. The power of the digital purse cannot be denied. If you want to reach this critical audience, you need digital marketing.

7. **Flexibility and convenience.** Web marketing is highly flexible if you invest in the right tools and experts. A website is much easier to edit than print marketing. You can run a Web or social media campaign for thirty days and then, based on metrics, stop the campaign and take your marketing strategy in a different direction. Changes can happen in real time and have immediate impact on your business. If a price change occurs at the last minute or if you want to run a quick special promotion, it's easy to make that happen with little additional cost.

8. **Make more sales.** Across industries, one fact remains consistent— you can and will convert new sales as a result of Web marketing. The percentage depends on how aggressively you market your inventory. Web marketing will increase your leads through information requests, emails, phone calls, and walk-in visits (if you have a physical office location). These leads are your pipeline for future sales. If you nurture and build a relationship with them, you can convert them into online and/or offline sales. I will cover how to build that relationship in future chapters. After approximately six months of serious online marketing, your sales will steadily grow. Your percentage of online sales out of total sales will depend on your lead follow-up and your level of commitment to on-going, consistent digital marketing.

9. **Look out for the little guy.** Web marketing was once relegated to

companies that could afford a corporate website costing several thousand to several hundred thousand dollars. Social media has completely changed that paradigm. Digital marketing is now available for even the smallest business. You can effectively market your business with a FREE Facebook page. You still need a website, but blogging makes building a website super easy and affordable. Even the smallest business can afford Web marketing today. If you demonstrate expertise and professionalism, you can appear much larger and more experienced online.

10. You don't have a choice. If you want to remain competitive, you must get on board. Google your company right now. Who comes up in your search results? Do you? Do your competitors? A website with no Web marketing is like a billboard in the Everglades. It doesn't exist. (I'm going to say this repeatedly in this book until it sinks in.) If your competitors are online, you have no choice. Get on board now while you still can or be forever left behind. Think about businesses that didn't adapt fast enough and went away, like phone books, VHS tape manufacturers, and pager companies. Yes, by putting your business online, your competition will know more about you. It's your job to know as much about them and deliver a much better experience to your customers than they can. Deliver a better product. Give better pricing. Offer fantastic customer service. Yes, they may pick up a few things from your website, but they can never replicate the essence of what makes your business the best.

I think what keeps most builders from building an effective online marketing strategy is not why they should do it, but rather how to do it. It's like many things we would like to change both personally and professionally. We know we should lose weight; we know we should stop smoking; we know we should cut up those credit cards or spend more time with our family, but we don't. Why? We don't know how to stop one behavior and replace it with a more productive one. The path is not clear. It seems hard. The risk of failure is too much.

The rest of this book is dedicated to solving the *how* problem you face with online marketing. If you are already sold on why you need digital marketing, then prepare to skyrocket your success and blow past your goals.

You Can Do This!

It stuns me that my young son can operate my iPhone better than I can. He downloads apps on our tablet and knows which one of our eight remote controls turns the DVR on and off. He connects to Hulu, controls the volume of the sound bar, and changes the channels on the TV. If he can already do all this at such a young age, what's next? Stephen-Spielberg-quality video productions with my iPad?

I did not grow up with technology. I know I appear extremely youthful (okay somewhat youthful) in my lovely photo, but the truth is, I know a really great photographer and a killer makeup artist. I may not be as young as you think. My first mobile phone was a *bag* phone for emergencies only. I also remember when fax machines first came out. You had to ask permission before you faxed someone, since using their ink and paper for frivolous reasons was a major offense.

My lightbulb moment about technology came while I worked as an HMO sales representative for United Healthcare. It was a tough job selling HMOs to doctors. I needed a new direction and I needed one fast. I heard about a brand new Master's Degree program at a prestigious private college in my town that married technology and communication. My dad told me there was something to that "Internet thing" and I should check it out.

I enrolled and was accepted. On my first day of graduate school at Rollins College, my professor issued me a laptop computer. My employer at the time had a mainframe system with proprietary software and I had never used a personal computer before. I hardly knew how to turn it on. I went home and spent the whole weekend unable to find any of the files I saved on the hard drive of my new laptop.

After watching me struggle—nearly in tears—my husband taped a note to the computer that read: *A = Floppy Disk and C = Hard Drive.* I didn't know the difference between my floppy disk and my hard drive. I enrolled in a $40,000 technology master's degree program and couldn't operate a basic laptop. All I knew was that I had to take the first step and catch up with the rest of the world. Maybe you are feeling the same way right now. Maybe you don't know exactly how to use social media effectively or design a website. The good news is you've found the right book and the right person to help you, just like the master's degree program helped me.

The very idea that several years later I would be a nationally-regarded expert, professional speaker, and owner of a Web marketing company was a foreign concept to me. The master's degree program helped me develop a passion for Web marketing. I couldn't learn fast enough. I graduated with a 4.0 GPA and was voted by my peers as the Most Outstanding Graduate Student in the class. I say this not to impress you, but to impress upon you that if you want to learn about technology and Web marketing, you can do this. With knowledge and practice you can learn the secrets to success just like I did. You might even find a passion for the subject.

You may not be computer savvy. You may hate Facebook and be completely against the idea of Twitter and tablets in the workplace. That's okay. Trust me. I can help you learn the skills to take your business where you want to go. Just keep reading.

Sound Familiar?

While conducting a full-day seminar with a group of home builders from around the country (who happen to all be male) on the do's and don'ts of website design, I heard a commotion coming from the audience. After several minutes of giggling and elbowing, someone finally spoke up to tell me what was so funny.

One of the builders in the group—in his haste to develop a Web presence for his company— registered his own name as the domain name without thinking through what his initials spelled. His name is Chris O. Jones, so he registered c-o-jones. That's right folks, it spells www.cojones.com. If you're not familiar with this term, it's a Spanish reference for part of the male anatomy. Chris was such a good sport that day and gave me permission to share his tale of woe with others.

Chris needed a marketing strategy—a comprehensive system that maps out the components, costs, and timeline resulting in sales. Such a strategy would have saved him a lot of money, time, and potential embarrassment.

If you are already a Web marketing believer, you probably relate to these questions:

- How many thousands of dollars have you wasted in marketing tactics that didn't increase traffic to your website?

- How many websites have you launched and had to redo because the site wasn't easy to update, didn't produce results, or changed webmasters?

- How many gurus have you hired and fired because they promised you a #1 ranking on Google but failed to produce results?

- How many social media seminars have you attended and walked away feeling confused?

- How many sales have you lost because you didn't follow-up on your leads?

You've probably learned the hard way by now that winging it on the Web does not work. After reading this book, you will have a working knowledge of Web marketing. You will be able to hire the right experts and hold them accountable. You will be able to devise a strategy that will save thousands of wasted marketing dollars and result in net new sales for your company.

I want you to feel empowered to take control of your Web marketing instead of relying on others who may or may not have your best interests at heart. You don't have to know HTML code to become an effective marketer. You need a conceptual understanding of how digital marketing can help your business grow.

CHAPTER 2

The Case for Strategy

MANY MARKETING professionals assume having a website is the same as having a digital marketing strategy. It is not. Just because you develop a website doesn't mean online shoppers can find it and when they do find it, will take action. Building a website is only the first step of an effective digital marketing strategy.

Another challenge professional digital marketers face is the DIY or do–it–yourself mentality. The attitude that anyone can do their own Web marketing, or hire a friend who builds and designs websites as a hobby, can be detrimental to your online sales strategy. Blogs, YouTube, and Facebook certainly make Web marketing much more accessible and DIY friendly, but developing your online strategy requires experience and expertise. Spend a little extra money to hire a marketing expert. You will recoup the investment in more online leads and sales.

A complete online marketing strategy begins with the end in mind. Think about what you want online visitors to do when they peruse your website? Do you want them to register for more information, follow you on social networks, sign-up for an email newsletter, download a brochure, or visit your model home/sales office? The first step is to identify and prioritize the action(s) you want visitors to take. Limit yourself to three main call-to-action goals. If you ask for too much, you will confuse and water down the effectiveness. That doesn't mean you can't offer other connection opportunities, but focus on promoting the top three.

In my opinion, your number one call-to-action goal is to drive in-person traffic. Websites don't sell homes. Relationships sell homes. Online shoppers buy from people they like and trust. Your website should compel online visitors to take the next step and visit your model home, sales office, or design center in person. The principal purpose of your digital marketing strategy is to align with your overall marketing plan and sales process to move prospects forward through each step.

The key to customizing your online strategy to meet your specific needs is to look at each step of the sales process and determine what tactics work best for your target market, budget, location, and goals.

The benefits of a strategic digital marketing approach include:

- Increased Return on Investment (ROI)

- Increased Competitive Edge

- Increased Traffic and Sales

1. Increase Your Return on Investment (ROI)

I've already mentioned that the dollars you spend on developing and implementing a comprehensive digital marketing strategy have a high return on investment. When done correctly, Web marketing is less expensive than traditional media, accelerates sales momentum, and yields net new sales.

The most difficult obstacle marketers face with Web marketing is doing it right the first time. A well-planned strategic approach to Web marketing saves precious time and money, increasing return on investment. Many marketers find themselves at the end of a website project only to discover the website can't be updated easily, was built in an outdated programming language, and won't accommodate future growth. Costly re-designs cause delays and eat away at your marketing budget. Other marketers discover in the months post-launch that the website does not produce information requests or sales. Since Web projects take a fair amount of time, effort, and money, starting over is not always possible. You then find yourself stuck with a tool that does not produce results.

Using an effective marketing strategy ensures you build a website as close to perfect as possible at launch, and builds-in the potential for easy updates and maximum flexibility, increasing ROI. Sales momentum is dramatically affected by your Web marketing strategy. Updating a website frequently with news and events, sending out email updates, and using blogs are just a few examples of how to create buzz about your product. The buzz translates into website traffic, requests for information, phone calls, and emails, which produces more onsite visits and eventually more sales.

2. Increase Your Competitive Edge

Thousands, millions, and possibly billions of other websites compete for your customers every day. Staying competitive today requires an innovative, multi-prong approach to drive online traffic. You also need a concentrated effort to maximize your website's influence on visit length and return visits. A digital strategy will help you determine, before building your website, how visitors will find you and what features will keep them coming back to learn more about your homes. We will explore several specific Web traffic drivers later in this section.

Driving traffic will keep you competitive. The huge competitive advantage lies in the conversion of online lead information requests to sales, via a well-executed lead follow-up process. You have the opportunity to gain market share, strengthen your brand, capture new sales, and fill a pipeline of future sales all by simply creating a disciplined, systematic, and consistent online lead follow-up program. We will explore this issue in-depth later in the section.

3. Increase Traffic and Conversion to Sales

Not only can a strategic approach save time and money, it can produce "net new" sales. How many net new home sales can you expect from Web marketing? It is hard to estimate because most buyers engage with more than one marketing source, so it is nearly impossible to determine the true Web-based driven sales. However, online activity from search to social media isn't slowing down. You can track your Internet sales effectively if you use a CRM (Customer Relationship Management) program, and code your website leads and ecommerce sales differently than your phone, print, and referral leads/sales. When one of those leads converts to a sale, you should count that toward your net new online sales. This percentage of sales is the most pure number you have access to in terms of Web-driven sales.

Are the sales you risk losing—because your product or service cannot be found online—not worth implementing a digital marketing strategy? Are the leads lost—because your presence does not compel action and/or you don't follow-up on the online lead request for more information—worth losing? **When you consider that Internet leads are less expensive to acquire, on average convert more quickly, and are more likely to be satisfied with their purchase, why wouldn't you want to spend the extra time and money developing a strategic Internet marketing plan?**

The Click Power System™

The Click Power System™ is a roadmap to a successful sales and marketing strategy. The system outlines five building blocks for success. You need all five to drive more traffic, online leads, and sales. This is not optional. You can't browse the five building blocks like a midnight buffet on a cruise ship and selectively pick one or two. You need them all.

The heart of this book is the synergy created by the five building blocks. Each one builds upon the next. Skip one and the Click Power System doesn't work. Take a look at Figure 1. Ask yourself which building block(s) you are missing, need to improve, or enhance?

Throughout the course of this book we will delve into each building block so you will learn the secrets of the system to increase your sales. There are plenty of options for you to decide how to execute each building block, but all five are required to achieve success.

Figure 1 – The Click Power System™

CHAPTER 3

Building Block #1
Your Website

The most important element of your Web marketing strategy is your website. **Think of your website like the foundation of a house.** It should be solid and sound before the next phase of construction begins. Don't waste time and money marketing a website that doesn't produce results.

What makes a website WOW? How do you know when you need a new website? First, let's establish how well your current site is performing.

Take a moment to answer the following questions:

1. How do prospective and current customers find your website?

2. How do they find you if they don't know your name?

3. How many unique visitors click through to your website each month?

4. What do most visitors do when they reach your website? Call? Register? Nothing? Don't know?

5. How many request info registrations or online leads do you receive per month?

6. How long do online visitors spend on your website?

7. How many pages do most visitors view?

8. What are the most popular pages of your website? Least popular?

You may not know the answers to these questions and that's okay. Most builders don't know, so you are not alone. The good news is that finding the answers is easy.

The answers are found in your website's analytic data. This information provides invaluable, objective feedback about the health of your website. Since the design component of website development is more subjective than objective, using website analytics neutralizes personal opinions and gives quantitative feedback about visitor behavior.

Think of Web analytics like an EKG for your website. Your website feeds valuable data to the analytics account, which organizes and compiles the data into meaningful feedback. If you currently do not use website ana-lytics, there are many providers that offer complimentary and fee-based analytic services. Search "website analytics" in your favorite search en-gine, and you will find plenty of providers to choose from. You can also talk to your webmaster about analytics programs he/she recommends.

I highly recommend adding Google Analytics to your website. This pro-gram is free and very easy to use. The reporting is robust and provides plenty of detailed information. Visit www.Google.com/Analytics to learn more and sign up for an account. If you already use Google for email or other programs, you can sign up and log in with your current Google username and password.

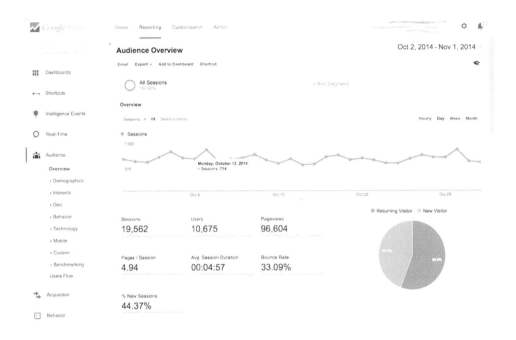

Figure 2 – Google Analytics Audience Overview Report

Just to be clear, Google Analytics tracks all your website traffic (not just the Google activity). If you are tech savvy, you can easily sign up for an account yourself. If not, ask your webmaster to set up an account for you. When you open a new account, Google Analytics provides a unique string of HTML code for your webmaster to embed in the footer of your website code.

After the code is installed, you can log in to your account anytime, day or night, and check your website statistics. You can also schedule automated reports emailed to you on a schedule you prefer (daily, weekly, monthly, etc.). Google Analytics is discussed more thoroughly in Building Block #5.

What Makes a Website WOW?

After reviewing hundreds of analytic reports for various-sized builders across the country, I noticed patterns about what works and what doesn't work for home builder websites. From those patterns, I developed the Builder Website Scorecard™ as an evaluation tool for effective website design and development. The Creating WOW website evaluation service is available for a fee, but through this book, you can review all the scorecard secrets for FREE.

To effectively use this scorecard, browse your favorite website as I describe each of the following components and compare that website to the criteria. You will find that the websites you prefer perform very well against the criteria—and that's what makes them so good.

The Builder Website Scorecard Criteria:

1. Content

2. Design

3. Navigation

4. Functionality

5. Experience

6. Call to Action

1. Content

Content refers to the copy, images, links, and multimedia used on the website. Think about content in terms of building a house. The more quality building materials you use, the higher the quality of the finished home. The same is true for websites. If you owned a retail store on pricey Madison Avenue, would you merchandise the window display with old, damaged mannequins wearing torn or worn-out clothing? No. You would place the best possible quality display in the window to attract traffic to come in the store and buy, buy, buy. The same is true for a website. Using amateur digital photographs and copy with grammar and spelling mistakes on your homepage is the equivalent of damaged goods in your display case.

In the digital world—and the real world—you get what you pay for. If you spend a little bit of money on high-quality graphics and images, you will reap big-time benefits in terms of online sales, online lead registrations, phone calls, and walk-in traffic. **Your homepage is your online model home.** Show off your homes for sale with the most breathtaking, eye-candy visuals you've got.

One of our most complimented website designs is the French Brothers website. French Brothers builds single-family homes in Alamogordo, Roswell, and Las Cruces, NM, starting from the $170s. One of the reasons the site receives so much praise is because of the simplicity of the design. The navigation bar is clean and uncluttered, and serves as a frame around their stunning photography. Because the photography is professional and high quality, we were able to use the pictures across the entire screen, creating an edge-to-edge design. This produces an instant impact and WOW effect as soon as the browser loads the page.

Figure 3 - www.FrenchBrothers.com

Photo and video content are the most popular types of content for Web visitors. If you are a builder, you should include an in-depth photo and video gallery on your website. Organize your photo gallery into albums by project name if you are a custom builder or remodeler, or by photo type such as exterior, interior, kitchen, bath, etc. Your video gallery can include testimonials, positive press, contractor interviews, design center tour, and available home tours.

The French Brothers homepage slideshow uses a mix of exterior photos, interior photos, and lifestyle photos. Don't make the mistake of showing only product photos on your website. Remember, buying a home is an emotional decision and the best way to appeal to emotion is to show photographs of homeowners enjoying the benefits of a new home. One of our home builder clients held a complimentary homeowner picnic and while everyone enjoyed hot dogs and hamburgers, a photographer took photos and video for their new website. The event resulted in plenty of customized lifestyle pictures and fantastic video testimonials, which really brought their new website to life.

You can also find high-quality lifestyle photos on stock photo websites such as gettyimages.com, istockphoto.com, and Fotolia.com. Just be sure to purchase the royalty free stock photos and check with your web designer for the correct photo size before you purchase. Stock websites charge by image size, so you don't want to overpay for larger images than you need or buy the photo twice. Typically, a homepage photo for a large slideshow requires at least a 1200 pixel image. Images that size can run from ten dollars to hundreds of dollars, depending on the photo you select.

Visually appealing content is important for the visitor's experience, but amount and quality of your text impacts your search engine rankings. To achieve a page one ranking, you need relevant, educational, value-added content in the form of HTML text. Google cannot index photos, videos, and images; they are essentially invisible to Google. Remember to think about your content in two parts: graphics that will wow potential home buyers, and HTML text for Google.

HTML text is text that is not embedded in a graphic or photo. If you aren't sure if your text can be indexed by Google, use your mouse and attempt to highlight the text. If you can highlight the text and copy it to a word document, then it is HTML text and can be indexed.

Another area where most home builder websites fall short is the amount of detail on the community, floor plan, available home, and home site pages. Include vivid descriptions and photos. While not all home buyers will take the time to read in-depth descriptions, it will improve your Google rankings. Embed important search terms into the copy with enough frequency so Google will index the page, but not so often that the copy is awkward and unappealing to visitors.

I am frequently asked if home builders should include pricing on their website. The answer is a resounding yes. Production builders should include specific base pricing per floor plan and exact available home pricing. Custom builders should include a price range of the size and scope of the custom homes built, with specific pricing on available home sites. Online shoppers expect to find pricing information during their online searches.

When it comes to copy, write conversationally and paint an emotional word picture. Your customers don't want to read your corporate brochure online. A great resource for website writing is *Letting Go of the Words: Writing Web Content that Works* by Janice Redish.[5] This book will teach you the nuts and bolts of writing for the Web.

Not only do you want to fill your website with great text and graphic content, it is important to make it easy to share the content. Social sharing buttons are easy to integrate and easy for visitors to simply click a Like button or Email a Friend to share content. One very good reason to encourage social sharing is it will boost your search engine rankings. We will discuss the importance of social interaction to search engine optimization in a later chapter.

Where should social sharing buttons be included? Main pages (the pages connected to the top navigation buttons) and product pages are ideal for social sharing integration. Blog pages and posts are also ideal.

There are several free social sharing integration services, and some even include tracking reports to monitor whether or not your content is being shared effectively. *Share This* and *Add This* are the two we use most frequently. If your site is based in Wordpress, there are numerous plugins for social sharing integration.

Content Checklist:

☐ Is your website content relevant to your target audience? Does the copy speak to the questions, concerns, fears, and hopes of your potential home buyers?

☐ Is your website content an appropriate quantity? Do you have enough HTML copy to make Google happy and enough visual graphics to make website visitors excited about your homes?

☐ Is your website content accurate and free of errors? Have you made sure the copy is grammatically correct and free of spelling errors and typos?

☐ Is your website content educational? Does your copy inform home buyers about the process of buying, financing, and building a home?

☐ Is your website content value-oriented? Does the copy sell new homes as a better value than a resale home? Does it visually demonstrate the benefits of your company?

2. Design

Design refers to the website's overall look. This is the trickiest area to evaluate because of the subjective nature of design; however, if you ask users within your target audience for feedback, you will receive helpful information about your website's design. **Remember, effective Web design isn't about what you like, it's about what your target audience likes.** As a starting point, keep these universal principles of website design in mind: 1) Designs should be clean and streamlined with plenty of white space to add balance; 2) Avoid dark backgrounds with reversed text that is difficult to read, especially for older eyes.

Also keep in mind that Web design trends change frequently. Dated website design is a red flag to visitors that your home designs might be outdated as well. First impressions online are just as important as first impressions offline. Don't turn off your visitors with a dated website design, photos, or videos. If the people in your lifestyle photos are wearing leg warmers, it's time to update your photos.

Why is clean Web design important? You don't want the website graphics to distract from the homes you are selling. It's the same rule we use in the world of professional dress: never let your outfit, makeup, hygiene, shoes, or accessories speak louder than your verbal message. Your website design should subtly sell your homes and support your brand message. Think of your website as a piece of art. The design represents the frame and the content represents the painting. The purpose of the frame is to enhance the painting so the observer can appreciate the art. It's the same with website design.

The Sego Homes website is a good example of clean design. Similar to French Brothers, Sego has a simple navigation bar with reversed text and icons to draw your eye to important buttons. The homepage slideshow pictures are large and rotate to demonstrate the quality and style of a Sego Home. The white background keeps the interior content pages clean and uncluttered.

Figure 4 – www.SegoHomes.com

When you design a new website, page layout is just as important as the color scheme and graphics. The page layout is your website's "real estate," so a highly-functional, flexible page layout will give you optimal spacing to highlight your content. Home builder websites are heavily data and image driven, with a lot of specific information to convey. A streamlined page layout will help guide the visitor's eye to the most important information.

The best resource by far on Web design is Steve Krug's book, *Don't Make Me Think*.[6] I highly recommend this book because Krug highlights a number of before and after website design examples with specifics on the changes.

An important challenge many builders face is how to design a website that renders properly and effectively on mobile devices and tablets. New websites built today should be built with responsive design, which allows the site to adapt to any device's screen size. If your existing website is more than a year old, it is probably not responsive. In that case, you most likely have a separate mobile website that you developed after the desktop version launched. The next time you build a new site, the desktop and mobile versions will be combined into one responsive site.

Design Checklist:

☐ Does your website have an emotionally compelling, professional, up-to-date homepage design?

☐ Does your website demonstrate consistent design throughout the website?

☐ Does your website appeal to your target audience with photos or graphics that represent their lifestyle?

☐ Does your website render properly and effectively on mobile and tablet devices?

3. Navigation

Navigation refers to the degree of ease that visitors click through your website. Navigation links should always be prominently displayed, clearly labeled, and easy to use.

Limit your primary navigation to no more than six buttons and your secondary navigation to no more than three buttons. Your navigation should funnel each visitor through your website on a strategic path toward an online sale, registration, live chat, phone call, and/or offline visit.

How do you decide the placement of your navigation? Start broad and narrow the funnel down with your content. Visitors should reach the most important information on your website from the homepage in one click. Offer multiple navigation buttons (drop-down menu, text link, radio button, check box, graphic banner) on each page. Amazon.com allows visitors to navigate their website brilliantly. Amazon provides many search paths to the same information so that virtually anyone can find what they want in a few seconds.

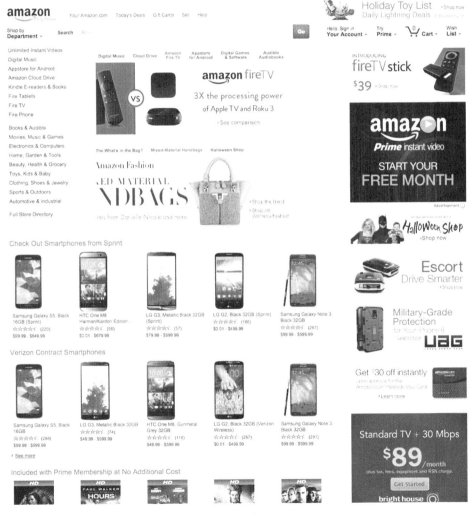

Figure 5 - www.Amazon.com

On Amazon.com, you can find a product in one click or less. That's impressive with thousands of products for sale. The secret to Amazon's ease of use are the numerous search refinement options available. You can search by broad keywords, topics, product type, author, title, etc. The more products available on your website, the more sophisticated your navigation must be.

When a potential home buyer visits your website, he/she wants to know three things in one click or less:

1. **What style and size homes do you build?**

2. **Where do you build?**

3. **How much are the homes and are any available now?**

If you bury this information on sub-pages below less important information, buyers will leave your website immediately. If you have multiple neighborhoods, a quick search on the homepage in the form of a map and/or drop-down menus is a great way to funnel buyers quickly to important information.

Once the home shopper is satisfied that you build homes at a price and location of interest, the next step is to learn more about your company. General content pages like About Us and Why Buy From Us become important once the home buyers decide they can afford your home in their desired location. The best way to prioritize your website content is to review the Top Content report in Google Analytics. This report will show you what pages had the most visits, longest visit length, and lowest bounce rate. In my experience, the Find Your Home, Available Homes, Floor Plan Gallery, and Photo/Video Gallery pages are the most visited pages of any home builder's website.

Navigation Checklist:

- ☐ Does your website use simple, user-friendly navigation? Is the navigation easy to use on a mobile device or tablet?

- ☐ Does your website allow home buyers to find a neighborhood, floor plan, available home, photo gallery, or home site in one click or less from the homepage?

- ☐ Does your website provide multiple search paths on each page to important information?

- ☐ Does your website provide strategic links in the copy to important information?

- ☐ Does your website provide navigation appropriate for your target audience?

- ☐ Does your website provide primary and secondary navigation?

- ☐ Does your website provide search refinement? Do you use maps, drop-down menus, or advanced searches?

4. Functionality

Functionality refers to the technical performance of the website. Visitors have little patience for slow downloads, broken links, and error messages. **At least once a month, complete a functionality review of your website.** Click on every button, link, and multimedia tool to make sure everything is working properly.

You should also test your website in different browsers. According to the numerous Google Analytics reports I review on a monthly basis, the top five most common browsers used are Safari, Chrome, Internet Explorer, Firefox, and Android. To confirm that your website is viewed correctly, check your Google Analytics report for the top browsers accessing your website and test accordingly.

Many times I've had a client tell me their webmaster swore their website looked fine in a browser and denied a problem. Always clarify what browser version the person is using before you try to convince them what the image looks like on your computer. If they are using a different browser, ask them to use your browser version for testing. If they refuse, you've got the wrong person for the job.

To avoid further confusion, always send a screenshot when you report a technical issue to your webmaster. Simply press the Print Screen button on your computer keyboard and then paste the image into your email. A screen capture will prove your case when the webmaster can't reproduce the problem. As much as your webmaster might want to help you, if the problem can't be reproduced, it can't be solved.

One of the biggest functionality issues home builders face is not on the front-end of the website (the part that potential home buyers see), but on the back-end (where changes are made to keep the website up-to-date). Unfortunately, many older websites do not have a user-friendly back-end CMS (Content Management System) that allows for in-house editing of the website by a non-technical person.

If this is the case, you should redesign your website with newer technology that allows for real time, in-house editing. It is so important that your content is timely, that you can't afford to wait for a Web designer to make the changes. CMS technology has vastly improved and even the most inexpensive website uses a simple CMS for easy editing. Of course, the more you want to edit your website yourself, the larger investment you will need to make in the CMS. However, the cost is worth every penny if you have the staff support ready, willing, and able to make changes. You will save thousands of dollars in change fees and, most importantly, save time on critical updates that might make or break a sale.

There are two types of CMS systems: open source and proprietary. Wordpress, Joomla, and Drupal are examples of Open Source CMS software. Open source means the software is free and developed by an open community of developers who make their code available online to anyone who wants to use it and integrate it into their website. The plus to open source CMS is that the price is right: FREE. The downside is that open source CMS code is hard to customize for more complex websites and, if the community of developers who support it stop, for whatever reason, you could end up with a CMS you cannot maintain. Of the open source CMS options, we recommend and use Wordpress.

Proprietary CMS software is developed by a private developer and is highly customizable to your needs. This type of software is easily integrated with other software, such as construction management and/or CRM (Customer Relationship Management) software, creating an end-to-end system that fully automates your business. Proprietary CMS software should have robust functionality and allow you to add/edit/delete unlimited pages, text, images, videos, and files to/from your website. You should be able to add/edit/delete community, floor plan, home site, and available home records. Make sure there is a blog module included in the CMS so you can easily update an integrated, fully-customized blog on your new website.

Other important features include:

- Administrative Controls – Set-up new CMS users with varying levels of access to the CMS.

- Form Management – Add/edit/delete forms, such as Contact Us or Warranty Request forms.

- Lead Management – Browse and export online lead reports.

- Log Viewer – Review CMS user activity by username.

- Mobile Management – Add/edit/delete content on your mobile website.

If you invest in a proprietary CMS, be sure to ask the Web developer if you own the source code and if you can move the website

to a new Web host if needed. Without the source code and the ability to move the website, you are locked-in with that developer for the life of the website.

When your new website finally goes live, there are several important pieces of information you need to document for future use. First, record your domain name, account user name, and password. Make sure the business owner is listed as the Administrative Contact on the domain name account. If you lose your account info, you can gain access if your name is on the account. If your webmaster is listed, the domain name company will only release the account information to your webmaster and not to you, which can be problematic if you part on bad terms or the webmaster goes out of business.

Second, ask your webmaster for the FTP (File Transfer Protocol), username, and password. With this information, you have a deeper level of access to the website than just the CMS username and password, which is helpful if you want to hire a new company to make changes to an existing website.

By asking for these items when the website goes live, you will avoid an awkward conversation later on that might be perceived negatively by the webmaster.

Functionality Checklist:

☐ Does your website load the homepage quickly, meaning in eight seconds or less?

☐ Does your website load photos, videos, and interactive elements quickly?

☐ Does your website label content clearly, meaning free of confusing industry acronyms or abbreviations?

☐ Does your website have a status graphic for downloads?

☐   Does your website allow for easy in-house editing and updating?

☐   Does your website render properly on mobile devices and tablets?

5. Experience

Experience refers to the degree a website entices visitors to interact on-line. Providing a great experience doesn't mean you need to spend a fortune on design bells and whistles for the sake of being *cool*. Whatever bells and whistles you add, such as video, music, or interactive games, should have a purpose that relates to the wants and needs of your target audience. If something has a purpose and it's really cool, that works just fine.

The purpose of interactive website features is to engage the visitor and keep them on your website longer, refer other visitors to your website, and/or return for new information. Examples of interactive features include:

- Interactive maps

- Interactive floor plans

- Customizable brochures

- My Favorites shopping cart

- Virtual tours

- Portfolio of past projects

- Photo gallery

- Video gallery

- Live Chat or Click-to-Call

- Interactive design studio

- Mortgage calculators

- White paper downloads

- Spanish or other language versions

A good example of how to create a memorable online experience in the home building industry is the website for Southport on Cape Cod, a fifty-five+ active adult community located in Mashpee, MA. Southport is a 250-acre, 750-home community, priced from the mid $300s. Amenities include 32,000 sq. ft. clubhouse, fitness center, grand ballroom, library, computer center, craft room, multiple pools, tennis courts, walking trails, nine-hole golf course, and many more. Developed by Ron Bonvie, a long-time Mashpee resident and experienced homebuilder/developer, this award-winning community is designed to provide the ultimate resort-style lifestyle.

Southport underwent a major website redesign in 2013 to build a new responsive design site that focused on more call to action and interactive elements. The website was designed and developed by Carlson Communications with consulting input by Creating WOW.

Cinematic visuals including panoramic photos and aerial videos, truly give website visitors a sense of place—the beauty and luxury of a Cape Cod retirement lifestyle.

The site features many interactive elements including an interactive site map, interactive floor plans, photo galleries, and video testimonials to keep visitors engaged.

1-800-840-7775 Follow us on Facebook   Schedule Your Tour ›

SOUTHPORT
CAPE COD, MA

Home Designs   Community   Lifestyle   Explore Cape Cod   Our Team   Contact

CAPE COD IS RENOWNED FOR
World-class Beaches

Best 55 and Over Communities in Massachusetts

Imagine a special place where neighbors come together as friends and friends come together as a family. A place where an unrivaled caliber of activities and amenities will be literally at your fingertips — making this the most active adult community you'll ever experience in New England. Now, stop imagining and start living the exceptional, award-winning lifestyle that is Southport – one of the premier 55 and over communities in Massachusetts!

12 New Home Sites Just Released! 9 New Homes Sold in October! View Site Plan

Southport TV Campaigns Feature Media Celebrities

Southport Developer Ron Bonvie, center, is joined by four New England media legends who describe what makes living at this national award-winning adult community so special. From left to right, Loren Owens and Wally Brine of WROR, Susan Wornick, former news anchor at WCVB-TV and Dan Rea, host of WBZ NewsRadio 1030's "NightSide with Dan Rea."

Figure 6 – SouthportOnCapeCod.com

Adding interactive elements will add to the overall cost of a website design project, so be sure your target audience will really appreciate the feature and that it supports your brand message. Interactive elements require top-notch graphics and images, so the first step to making your website more interactive is to first produce high quality floor plan, elevation, and site map photography and/or renderings.

Interactive elements are particularly effective in explaining complex processes, such as design studio selections or green construction features. A well-designed interactive graphic will convey detailed information much more effectively than multiple paragraphs of text. You can always include the text below the graphic for SEO purposes.

Again, don't become fixated on having a particular feature just because you think it's cool.

Experience Checklist:

☐ Is your website compelling to your home buyers?

☐ Is your website more engaging than your competition?

☐ Does your website integrate features that allow the visitor to personalize their experience?

6. Call to Action

Using both text and graphics that compel visitors to call, click, check out more of your products, or come by your office is called a Call to Action. Websites are active sales vehicles if they ASK visitors to engage. An example of a website with over-the-top call to action is GoDaddy.com. A good exercise is to count the number of calls to action on one page of GoDaddy.com and then count the number on your own website. While you may not want as much as GoDaddy.com, strive for three to four calls to action per page.

The redesign of the Southport on Cape Cod website is an excellent case study on how adding call to action to a website can dramatically increase leads, tours, and sales.

The Southport website prior to the redesign in 2013 was an award-winning design. The design focused on selling lifestyle, and it complimented the sales center and collateral materials. Despite the appealing look and feel of the website and aggressive marketing, the website was only converting 1.2 percent of Unique Visitors (measured in Google Analytics) to Internet Leads (Request Information form completion and/or eNewsletter sign-up).

What is the standard lead conversion for home builder websites? Your website should convert 2 to 5 percent of your monthly Unique Visitors to Internet Leads. How did we determine what was limiting the lead response? We took a deep dive look at the website's Google Analytics reports.

The new website has ten to twelve call to action opportunities per page including:

- Toll-free number for inquiries

- Multiple social media links

- Schedule Your Tour

- Request a DVD

- Newsletter Sign-Up

- Request Information

- Live Chat

- Social Sharing

- Watch a Video

- View Site Plan

- Ask a Homeowner

Even though home builder websites are not literally selling a product online, you should still think like an ecommerce website. Merchandise your website with action language to encourage visitors to call you, visit an onsite location, or register online for more information.

One of the biggest mistakes home builders make is failing to treat their website like a store. A website doesn't have to be a passive brochure that just costs money to develop and maintain. It can be an ACTIVE sales vehicle that generates leads which, when properly managed, can develop into offline sales.

The number of online sales calls and/or online leads you receive is a direct correlation to the strength of your call to action language and graphics.

Tips to improve your website's calls to action:

- Set aside room on every page for a promotional area that is updated frequently. In this area, promote a featured home/home site/neighborhood/floor plan, price discount, incentive, or contest/sweepstakes.

- Use graphic buttons/banners with action language to grab visitors' attention, such as Learn More, Sign Up, Start Here, and Get It Now.

- Include a short email sign-up form on every page.

- Offer visitors a toll-free number to call for more information, and post it in the same place on every page in a highly visible location.

- Offer Live Chat or Click-to-Call technology on your website to encourage visitors to interact instantly while they are on your website.

- On every page, add text links to your online store and/or the Contact Us page. Use sales language and invite visitors to buy or register today. Ask and you shall receive.

- Offer an incentive/discount for online visitors in exchange for a purchase or registration.

- Keep your Contact Us form short. Limit the required fields to name and email address.

Live Chat is one of the best calls to action for a home builder website. Live chat produces high quality leads by allowing visitors to chat instantly. If you average a minimum of 1,000 visits a month to your website, then you can benefit from Live Chat. There are two forms of Live Chat: hosted and do-it-yourself. Hosted Live Chat allows you to outsource to a call center that monitors your website and responds to requests on your behalf. You provide a script and they will turn that chat request into a lead as quickly as possible. Hosted Live Chat is very effective since it provides consistent coverage on the website and operators are highly trained on lead conversion.

Do-it-yourself Live Chat is less expensive (can be as little as $40/month) and can work if you have someone available in your office during peak website traffic times. Your in-house operator will need Live Chat training to maximize the lead conversion. DIY chat is generally not as effective as Hosted Chat because the in-house operator might not be available online for nearly as many hours a day and days of the week as the hosted operator.

Call to Action Checklist – Does Your Website:

☐ Define the next step for visitors?

☐ Ask the visitor to purchase, register, call, or visit in person?

☐ Have a short registration form?

☐   Have an email sign-up form on every page?

☐   Use promotional graphic buttons/banners?

☐   Offer Live Chat and/or Click-to-Call options?

☐   Offer an incentive in exchange for registration or purchase?

☐   Offer a toll free number prominently displayed on every page?

☐   Use an interactive map to provide directions to offline locations?

How well did your website score? If it didn't score as well as you would like, don't worry. **The average shelf life of a website is two to three years since technology advances so rapidly.** The website will be due for an update soon, even if recently launched. A brand new website is never finished. A website is an organic entity. It evolves as your business evolves. Budget marketing dollars every year toward the improvement of your website and you will gain a significant competitive advantage.

CHAPTER 4

Building Block #2
Drive Traffic

Now that you have an effective Web presence, you need to drive traffic to your website. Don't assume that because you built a website, customers will find you. If a tree falls in the forest and no one hears it, did it really fall? If you have a website and no one can find it, does it really exist?

Promoting your website and, ultimately, your homes for sale, requires a mix of marketing tools. Just like you use specific tools for specific tasks when building a house, you use specific marketing tools for specific goals.

Marketing tools are typically broken into two categories: inbound and outbound.

Inbound marketing tools *pull* visitors to you who have an interest and are an ideal fit for your product or service. These tools include search engine marketing, content marketing, blogging, social media marketing, and permission-based email marketing.

Outbound marketing tools *push* your message out to attract attention for your service or product. These tactics include print advertising, signage, direct mail, television, and radio advertising. They tend to be more expensive than inbound tools, and it is more difficult to measure return on investment. The use of outbound marketing tools has lessened in recent years with the rise of inbound marketing, but there are still appropriate uses for these tools in the marketing of new homes. What is important is that you get the right mix for your target audience, product type, and market.

In addition to inbound and outbound marketing tools, builders should also look at special promotions, event marketing, and public relations as potential ingredients in the marketing mix.

How do you know what to include in your marketing mix? I highly recommend the National Association of Home Builders, Institute of Residential Marketing (IRM) courses to learn how to determine your target market. You should not invest in a marketing tactic until you are sure it will be effective with your audience. The IRM courses teach in-depth how to determine, reach, and influence your target market. The curriculum consists of two courses. Each course has one day of online learning and one day of classroom learning. The courses have been newly updated and are highly relevant to current marketing and consumer trends.

After you have defined your target audience, you can effectively map out your marketing tactics. Think of your marketing strategy like a wagon wheel. At the center of the wheel is the hub. The hub connects to the wheel via spokes. Your website is the hub of your sales and marketing strategy. Once it is in place, you need several traffic drivers to lead visitors to your hub. This is where the strategy comes into play. You want to carefully select the right marketing tactics as your traffic drivers.

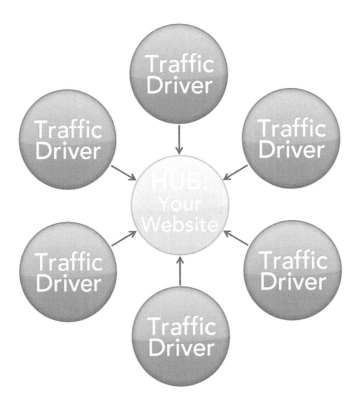

Figure 7 – Meredith's Wagon Wheel of Marketing Strategy

In addition to understanding the needs and desires of your target market, you also need to understand the pros and cons of each traffic driver option. The subsequent chapters describe each option in simple terms and provide you with a working understanding of how each driver works, plus the costs and benefits of each option.

After you understand your options, the next step is to select the options that most align with your sales objective, budget, and online marketing skill set. I firmly believe that some options are better than others, depending on the company's comfort level with technology. There is nothing wrong with that approach. Utilize your strengths.

Finally, you have to deploy these strategies and measure the results. This will require ongoing reviews and tweaking of tactics. Like any marketing, digital marketing is never finished, complete, or final. It is an organic process that can easily flex, grow, and change as your business grows.

In this book we are going to focus on the following online marketing tools:

- Search Engine Optimization (SEO)

- Paid Search Marketing (PPC)

- Referral Websites

- Online Display Advertising and Behavioral Targeting

- Online Public Relations

- Social Media Networks

- Content Marketing

We will review the pros and cons of each of these traffic-driving options in the next section. First, we start with Search Engine Optimization.

Search Engine Optimization
The Secrets AND Lies of Page One Rankings

Search engine optimization, or SEO, is the process of improving a website's rankings in the organic or free listings of a search engine. The organic search results appear below the Sponsored Search Results and Local Results on most search engines. Search engine marketing is one of the most effective inbound marketing tools to drive targeted traffic to your website.

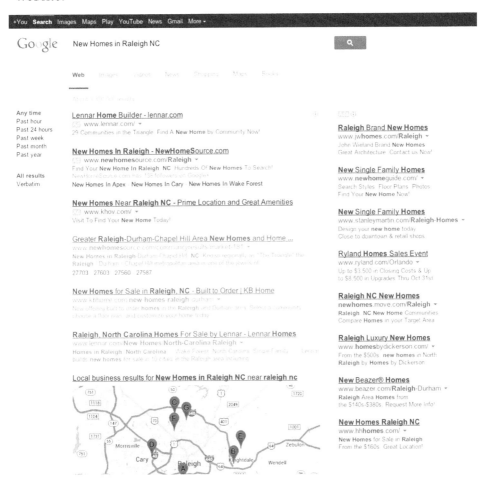

Figure 8 – Google Organic Search for "New Homes in Raleigh NC"

Free listings are referred to as *organic* because the search engines claim these results are the natural or best match to your search. Even though you don't pay a search engine directly to rank in the organic results, you will need to make a monthly investment with a search engine marketing firm to achieve page one rankings.

Organic search listings are highly competitive and you must rank well on page one or two for customers to effectively find your website. In my experience, online searchers almost always click on a result from the first page. Most don't even look past page two, and certainly not past page three, for answers to their searches.

How do search engines work? Think of a search engine like a phone book. Search engine *spiders* crawl the web categorizing websites, trying to determine where to place each website in the virtual phone book. The spiders look at both your back-end code and your front-end copy to determine where your website belongs in the phone book. Do you belong in AC Repair or Health Clubs? If a search engine can't determine where you belong in the phone book, they won't rank your website at all.

Why the big fuss about SEO? A Pew Internet survey[7] found that 91 percent of Americans use a search engine when looking for more information, and that 78 percent use a search engine to research more information about a product or service before purchasing.

The search engine you want to concentrate on is Google. According to a comScore April 2014 report, Google leads the search market with 67.5 market share. To put this in perspective, Microsoft search sites have 18.6 percent of the market, followed by Yahoo at 10.1 percent.[8] Since Google has the largest percentage of searches, this is where you should focus your time and budget. The bad news is that Google is the hardest search engine to optimize. The good news is that it isn't impossible. It can be done.

One of my favorite resources to learn more about SEO is SearchEngine-Land.com.[9] I find the content well-written and current. The website is easy to navigate and they have tons of FREE articles and whitepapers you can download to learn more about SEO and why it's important.

How often does Google index your website? Google looks at a website every couple of weeks. If you update your website with new content that clearly defines your category in the phone book, your website's positioning increases. Conversely, if a change on the website negatively impacts Google's ability to categorize your content, the positioning decreases.

If you want to know when Google last visited your website, Google your website and click on the small arrow next to your URL. A drop-down menu will appear. Click on the Cached text link. This will bring up a snapshot of your page. Located at the top is the date Google last indexed the page. The page will appear the way Google saw it and highlight any key words. Now Google a popular keyword for your industry. Look at the number one listing. Click on the Cached link. Notice how many keywords are highlighted on the page. Keyword density is very important to Google.

I don't want to oversimplify here. There is a complex formula to Google rankings and it changes regularly. Keyword density is only one part of the equation. There are several important factors, including:

- Title and description tag optimization

- Alt tag optimization

- Quantity and quality of text content

- Website popularity and traffic

- Quantity of inbound, relevant links

- Website ease of use and conversion rate

- Degree of social interaction

- Website ease of use and functionality

- Few technical errors/broken links

- Mobile/tablet friendliness

Achieving a desired ranking on Google requires a big picture approach to SEO. The most important aspect of the process is using the right key-words. You can spend a lot of time and money optimizing your website, only to find out the keywords you chose don't bring enough traffic and/or the wrong traffic to your website. Our keyword strategy at Creating WOW strives to balance high quality relevant keywords with keywords that have a high search volume that will drive a lot of traffic.

Another mistake home builders make is to insist on keywords based only on their personal search habits. No two people click the same way. A pro-fessional SEO firm can pull a report of keyword phrases by search volume. This will provide you with an unbiased look at which phrases are really searched and which ones aren't. This is critical information and should be considered carefully.

How many keywords should you pursue? Some SEO firms will pursue fifty or more phrases, which is called the "long-tail" approach. These firms will build many landing pages pointing back to the main website. Other firms will concentrate on a few phrases at a time and optimize the main website with those to achieve desired positioning and build out the website from there. Neither approach is right or wrong and should be applied on a case-by-case basis, depending on your brand's needs.

Participation in social networks is vital to improve your search engine rankings. Google+ is Google's social network and their attempt to compete with Facebook. Companies that have a regularly updated and relevant Google+ page rank well in search results, especially if the page has a high degree of fan interaction. Google+ users actually see different search results than non-users because Google uses data from their profile to further personalize search results. If a Google+ user gives your website a +1 (equivalent to a Like on Facebook), your website will rank at the top of page one for that user anytime they search for you. That's a huge incentive to start interacting on Google+ with your customers.

Google+ isn't the only social network that can help boost your Google organic positioning. Participating on websites like LinkedIn, Twitter, and Facebook is very beneficial because Google indexes those pages just like it indexes your website. In certain cases, your business Facebook page will appear higher in the search results than your corporate website. Consumers also want to know what their friends have to say about you in addition to your corporate sales pitch. The more social networks you and your company participate on, the more possible search listings you will have. One of our builder clients actually dominated the entire first page of Google search results between their corporate website, blog, Facebook page, Twitter profile, online press releases, YouTube videos, and LinkedIn profiles. Your company could do the same.

Quick tips to improve your search engine rankings:

- Use keyword-rich HTML text on every page of your website.

- Regularly add valuable, keyword-rich content to your website.

- Seek out highly-relevant, non-paid, inbound links to your website.

- Limit optimization to a couple of keyword phrases per page.

- Research your keyword phrases carefully, and select phrases that are highly trafficked, but have little competition from other websites.

- Offer a quality visitor experience on your website.

- Ask others to recommend your website on social bookmarking sites and social media networks.

- Update your title, keyword, and description meta tags on every page of your website.

- Tag all of your images with keyword-rich alt tags instead of generic descriptions.

- Tag all of your URLs and hyperlinks with keyword tags called permalinks.

- Review your website analytics for the keywords and search phrases most commonly used to find your website.

- Use an HTML sitemap on your website and use an XML sitemap file.

- Use heading tags appropriately, specifically the H1, which is generally used as the Page Title.

- Be aware of rel=nofollow for links. This tells Google not to follow certain links on your site.

- Use robots.txt. This tells Google whether they can access and crawl parts of your website. Place in the root directory.

- Use Google Webmaster tools to identify problems and troubleshoot issues.

- Participate in social networks, such as Facebook, YouTube, and Twitter. Link from these popular websites to your website.

SEO requires the use of an outside firm. Choose one wisely. Many claim to be experts, but few truly are. There is a big difference between a website design expert and an SEO expert. One does not automatically equal the other. In fact, the two disciplines often find themselves at odds with one another because what's best for the visitor experience isn't always what's best for SEO. The best approach is to prioritize the visitor experience as most important and SEO as secondary. Nothing should hinder the visitor experience so that visits turn into leads and/or online sales. If a company wants to change your website and negatively impact the visitor experience, decline and understand it may affect your rankings slightly. Ultimately, what good are rankings if your website doesn't convert leads into sales?

Ask the SEO firm to give references and assess how they stay up-to-date on changes. Ask the firm to provide a sample report and ask how often you would meet to review results. Don't expect the SEO program to run on autopilot. You can't measure what you don't manage. You need to drive the project and hold the firm accountable for results. Be willing to meet at least once a month and ask questions. It doesn't matter if you feel you don't know a lot about the subject. Much of this discipline is common sense; you know more than you think.

What should your expectations be? It can take several months to see a change in your rankings. The more competitive the keyword phrase, the longer it will take to improve your results. It is also important to focus on the right results. SEO isn't all about ranking #1 on Google. Seriously. What you really want to achieve is an overall increase in organic search engine traffic. This is easy to measure in Google Analytics.

You will also begin to see an increase in your overall traffic within a month or two—long before you actually see improved rankings. Some business owners forget the forest for the trees with SEO. Don't become hung up on rankings and fail to miss the overall picture that traffic is improving, online lead requests are increasing, and sales are up.

You should also expect to see your rankings fluctuate. **Don't Google yourself every day.** It will only frustrate you. Remember Google indexes every couple of weeks, so a daily check is a waste of time. Your rankings will change. Why? Ask Google. No, seriously. You will fluctuate because this isn't a static competition. Every website is a moving target. If your competitor is indexed and has optimized their website, they might move ahead of you until the next time you are indexed.

What does SEO cost? It totally depends on the competitive nature of your market and keywords. You can do a one-time sweep of your website to have it fully optimized, which will help you in the short term. However, SEO is an ongoing commitment since search engines frequently change the rules and algorithms.

Expect to spend at least $1,000 – $2,000 a month for a reputable search firm. Depending on your market and competition, you could spend tens of thousands of dollars on SEO. Did I just scare you off? Don't worry. If that's too much for your budget, consider Paid Search instead. You can set your budget and receive commensurate results for Paid Search. With SEO, if you don't spend enough to improve your results, you may not receive ANY results at all.

Why is SEO so expensive? Because it is very labor-intensive. You are buying hours on a monthly basis and your budget dictates how many hours you receive. The more hours available, the more work is done on each page of your website (known as onsite optimization), and more content can be created and shared. Once that is complete, the offsite optimization begins with link-building campaigns and social media. In addition to labor costs, there are costs for managing the project, reporting, and meetings to review progress. All of this requires a magic mouse operated by people who are highly skilled and knowledgeable.

If you see your website as a permanent fixture in your business plan, which you should, and you are in business for the long haul, then SEO is absolutely a must for you. You just need to find the right partner and work together to track and measure the progress of your website.

Paid Search
Pay To Play

The next Internet marketing option is Paid Search, also known as Pay-Per-Click (PPC), Google AdWords, search engine marketing (SEM), or Sponsored Search Marketing. Even though PPC is technically paid advertising, most marketing experts place it in the inbound marketing category. The ability to target your message to an audience specifically looking for your product or service makes it an inbound marketing tool. Home builders who use PPC marketing incorrectly and place ads without proper targeting, are using it as an outbound marketing tool and will not see the same results.

Figure 9 - Google Pay-Per-Click Search Results for
"New Homes in Raleigh NC"

It is easy to be included in the Paid Search results. Open an advertising account with the search engine of your choice, select your keywords, write the ads, give them your credit card number, and a maximum monthly spend amount. In less than twenty-four hours your ad is up and running. It is an easy and FAST way to create a presence on the search engine. **With Paid Search, if you PAY, you PLAY.** Your website also doesn't have to be search-engine-friendly or even user-friendly to use Paid Search

With Paid Search, you bid in an e-Bay auction-like system for positioning. Let's say you want the #1 position in the Paid Search results for the keyword phrase *New Homes in Orlando*. In your account, place a bid amount for that phrase. If your bid is the highest, your ad is placed in position #1. The second highest bid is position #2, and so on.

If someone clicks on your ad, the bid amount is debited from your account. You can limit your exposure by placing a maximum spend amount per twenty-four-hour period. If you bid $2.00 per click for position #1 of the keyword phrase *New Homes in Orlando* and you set a $10.00 per day spend limit, then after five clicks, your ad is removed until the following day.

The key to Paid Search is to find highly targeted keyword phrases that are affordable per click and highly searched. A phrase that costs only ten cents per click may seem like a bargain, however, if only five people searched it last month, you won't receive much traffic to your website. The keyword strategy is where a professional paid search management expert can really help maximize your return on investment.

Like SEO, Paid Search requires ongoing maintenance and monitoring. However, Paid Search is DIY (Do-It-Yourself) friendly, if you have a savvy online marketing person and you invest in initial training and set-up. Also, like SEO, it is imperative you use the right list of keywords from the beginning. Like most things, you will get what you pay for in both SEO and PPC. If you are considering a Paid Search budget of more than $500/month, invest in a professional digital marketer with PPC management experience. He/she can stretch $500 much further than you can by getting more clicks for less money.

Paid Search really is an art form. To find a great firm specializing in PPC, look for a company that is Google AdWords certified or has documented paid search experience. Certification indicates the company conducts Paid Search campaigns regularly, and those campaigns meet a certain budget threshold. Professional paid search experts will create multiple versions of your ad and split test them to find the best response. They will also create customized landing pages per ad to increase your lead conversions and know how to research new keyword phrases that you (and probably your competition) have yet to discover.

You can log in to your Paid Search account any time and monitor the amount of traffic, bid prices, and total spend amount. I recommend checking the keywords and bid prices at least once a week and then once a month. In your account, you can view your campaign, edit your account settings, pull tracking reports, and edit your ad. One of the best uses for AdWords is the geo-targeting features. You can target areas to include and even exclude certain areas. This maximizes your budget and increases your ROI.

If you aren't using Paid Search, I recommend you start with Google AdWords. If you want to expand, advertise with Bing and Yahoo Paid Search. If you participated in all three, you would see a huge increase in your traffic since those search engines power the Paid Search listings for several other search engines.

The budget for Paid Search varies widely. Our home builder clients spend anywhere from $500/month to $3,000+/month. You can spend as little or as much as you want to spend. There are no contracts, so you can turn it on and off at will. The cost per click depends on the size of the market and how much competition there is for your keywords. The more people bidding on a phrase, the higher the cost per click will be for the best position.

You don't always want to be #1 in Paid Search Sometimes it's best to pay as little per click as possible. As long as the monthly budget is used up each month, who cares if you do that at position #4. It is smarter to shoot for more clicks than pay more for fewer clicks. If you have an unlimited budget, then go for #1.

Many people tell me they don't think anyone clicks on the Paid Search ads because they know they are ads. There are consumers who are aware of the ads, but many are not. You will receive a monthly report from Google AdWords that shows you exactly how many clicks you received. Keep in mind that you only pay if someone clicks on your ad. So if no one clicks on the ad, no harm, no foul. Trust me, after reviewing these reports for clients through the years, I can tell you plenty of people click on Paid Search Ads.

The bounce rate (number of people who only view one page of your website) is usually slightly higher for AdWords than Search Engine Optimization. The cost does increase over time as you and your competitors drive the bid prices up for certain keywords. For those reasons, I usually recommend Paid Search as a short-term strategy until your SEO kicks in, or for the purpose of pushing a specific short-term campaign. Another use of Paid Search is if you don't have control of your website and SEO is not an option. I have found in many cases Paid Search is better for custom builders than SEO because it produces more traffic more quickly. SEO for custom builders is okay, but on many occasions it doesn't produce enough additional traffic to justify the investment.

Click fraud (someone clicking on your ads over and over just to run out your budget) is an issue that concerns some businesses. If you are really concerned about it, you can hire a service to monitor your clicks and alert you to potential fraud. In my experience, I have not seen any major cases of click fraud, and in minor instances Google notified us of the issue and refunded the account.

Paid Search Tips:

- Monitor your keyword phrases and bids weekly.

- Review your website analytics report and look for trends and key-words producing the best results.

- Spend enough money to make a difference. Don't think you can spend $50/month and see a huge increase in traffic.

- Bid on misspellings of your own company name, products, and services.

- Test multiple versions of your paid search ad and see which one receives the most clicks.

- Create specific landing pages custom tailored to your paid search ad.

- Use a phone number tracking system to track the number of phone calls your ads generate.

- Offer Paid Search visitors a special offer just for them. This will help you track results and increases the number of leads.

Which is better, SEO or Paid Search? It really depends on your goals. If you want a fast, easy, DIY option, then Paid Search is the best one for you. If you don't like the idea of bid prices increasing over time, the potential for click fraud, AND you are patient, then SEO is a better option for you. Of course, nothing says you can't do both and many companies do.

Local Search Is the New National

Have you noticed Google search results with red balloons that correspond with a map in the right sidebar? These listings are local search results. They are Google's answer to the online yellow pages and provide local brick and mortar options for your search results. **Local search visibility should be an important component of your search marketing program.** Local searches are quickly outpacing Google.com searches of Web users looking for local businesses to purchase a good or service.

Figure 10 - Google Local Search Results for
"New Homes in Raleigh NC"

Originally, the local listings on Google were referred to as Google Places. Google then merged Google Places with Google+ Business Pages. Today, local search results including search, map and Google+ are managed in one dashboard called Google My Business, found at www.google.com/business/.

If you previously used Google Places for Business or Google+ Pages Dashboard to manage your business information, your account has been automatically upgraded to Google My Business. From your Google My Business account, you can edit your contact information, business description, hours, directions, phone number, website URL and more.

In order to add a business to Google My Business, you must have a mailing address and meet the quality guidelines. If you want to create a business page without an address, then create a Brand page instead of a local Google+ business page.

Once you set up the local Google+ business page, it is important you have it officially verified with Google. The verification process can be done by phone or postcard. For the phone option, you have to be able to directly answer the phone number listed on the Google+ business page to receive the verification code. For the postcard option, you must be able to receive mail at the address listed on the page to receive the postcard with the verification code. Whichever process you chose, once you have the verification code simply enter it into your Google My Business dashboard.

Now that the basics of your page are complete, you want to add photos and copy to fill out your page. Use SEO keywords and hash tags throughout the copy on your Google local page that compliment your SEO strategy. You should also solicit reviews from customers for your Google local page. The page with the most and best reviews will rank number one in the local search results.

Referral Websites
The Mall of the Internet

Referral websites are also an excellent way to be found online. Many of these will aggregate real estate listings into one portal website. For example (in alphabetical order): homes.com, move.com, newhomedirectory.com, newhomeguide.com, newhomesource.com, realtor.com, trulia.com, and zillow.com. Other referral websites aggregate ratings and reviews of local businesses. For example: AngiesList.com, Houzz.com, Porch.com, and ServiceMagic.com. Think of a referral website like an online mall, gathering similar businesses together into one convenient place so consumers can quickly scan the listings and reviews to compare and select their favorite products.

Figure 11 - www.NewHomeSource.com

Some referral websites are free (i.e. Craig's List) and some charge a monthly or per click fee. Ask a lot of questions about fees and make sure you understand the structure of the referral website before you sign up. If a website has free and paid listing options, know that the free listings are generally buried so far down the search results that they won't generate many leads or drive much traffic to your website. Invest in the premium listings and your results will be much more satisfactory.

If you are considering a free referral website that is not industry specific, such as Craig's List, buyers beware. Sometimes you get exactly what you pay for. Free referral sites are not a bad idea, but you should NOT rely on them as your main source of traffic. These non-specific referral websites lack targeting and quality control. Some may also post questionable material that you may not want your products or brand associated with. Research and do your homework before you participate on a free referral site.

By listing your homes on a high-quality referral website, you can receive instant traffic. Highly-qualified online leads will visit your website and increase your brand's visibility. Many of these websites are well-positioned in search engines. This increases your website's visibility. Referral websites also give your website credibility since consumers view them as a third-party endorsement. Online leads generated from referral websites are incredibly valuable because the consumer looked at the entire database of listings and still chose you.

Referral websites are an excellent, low-maintenance way to list your homes. Another advantage of referral websites is their excellent search engine positioning for organic results, which provides high volumes of visitors and leads for your website.

Many of the referral websites can automatically feed your listings from your website to their site and eliminate manual data entry and maintenance. You can subscribe to a feed service like NewHomeFeed.com or build a feed directly into your website CMS. The advantage of a feed service is greater distribution. Your listings will appear on many referral sites. If you want to select specific referral sites and have greater control, then building a feed into your website CMS is a better option.

Online Display Advertising and Behavioral Retargeting Ads

Look At Me, Look At Me!

Also known as banner advertising, Online Display Advertising is an outbound marketing option. **Banner ads are best used on highly-targeted and industry-specific referral websites such as NewHomeSource.com or Move.com.** Run the campaign in short bursts with a specific offer and strong call to action. Banner ads are not as effective for generic branding purposes as they are at generating interest in a specific promotion or incentive. Make sure the banner ad clicks through to a specially designed landing page with a short capture form to maximize your ROI.

Banner advertising results are measured in click-throughs (CTR), which is the percentage of visitors who clicked on the banner and transferred to your website and impressions, which is the number of views a banner receives. Pricing is generally determined by CPM (cost per thousand) impressions the banner will generate on the referral website. For best results, use clever, eye-catching content and refresh every thirty days.

The problem with banner ads is that online shoppers try to avoid *push* advertising. To succeed at this type of advertising, make sure you have a clear goal supplementing additional online marketing efforts. Banner ads should never be your main traffic driver.

A more advanced banner marketing strategy is to use behavioral targeting known as audience targeting technology. With audience targeting, your website embeds a unique cookie on the visitor's browser and then collects data on each visitor as they browse your website. Information is fed back to a database, which then deploys your banner ad on a network of websites so the visitor continues to see your ad after they leave your website. This creates multiple brand impressions and increases the chance of a conversion. It feels a little like *big brother*, but it's a very common marketing practice.

We recommend behavioral targeting ads on Facebook and the Google content network. Our clients have seen good quality traffic (measured by length of visit on the site and bounce rate) from these two platforms. Behavioral targeting banner ads in the Google content network are set-up and managed within Google Adwords. Facebook behavioral ads can be set-up directly on Facebook or through a third-party website like AdRoll.

Online Public Relations
Incredible Value & ROI

Organizations use online public relations as a vehicle to communicate with the public. Managing the attitudes, opinions, and perceptions of your target audience is a daunting practice best accomplished with public relations. The Web provides a whole new venue for your public relations program. Many free PR websites will post your press releases. **The benefits of online public relations include: increasing your brand exposure, building high-quality relevant inbound links to your website, and any subsequent media coverage about your project.** PR is the most powerful form of marketing because it delivers information from an unbiased third party, improving your organization's credibility.

Online public relations work best when you have truly newsworthy information to share. Hire a professional public relations writer or firm to determine what is newsworthy, write the press release, and distribute to both online and offline sources. Make sure you include your website's address in the press release and any other relevant links. Remember to post the press release on your own website too.

If you are a small business just starting a public relations effort, you may want to start with free press release distribution websites. Be aware that you will not make the same impact with a free press release website as a paid service. Free sites tend to take more effort to create the post and they don't always post immediately.

Paid press release distribution sites reach more people and have advanced features like video, images, hyperlinks, and social media links. They have more targeted distribution and better search engine optimization value. Paid sites also generally send your press release to their press list as well as posting on their own website.

Nobody uses press releases to solely capture the media's attention any more. Today, online press releases are more about communicating directly with your audience. I highly recommend David Meerman Scott's, *The New Rules of PR*.[10] It really opened my eyes to the value and power of online PR.

Free Press Release Website Options:

- Scribd.com

- Storify.com

- Newsvine.com

- Scoop.it

- Calameo.com

- DocStoc.com

- PRLog.com

- Sulia.com

- OpenPR.com

- NewsWireToday.com

- Free-Press-Release.com

- SBWire.com

- Kontax.com

- PressReleaser.org

- MyPRGenie.com

- BeforeItsNews.com

- PRFire.co.uk

- 1888PressRelease.com

- Newsbox.com

- OnlinePRNews.com

- Wesrch.com

- PitchEngine.com

- Pressbox.co.uk

Paid Press Release Website Options:

- PRWeb.com

- eReleases.com

- 24-7PressRelease.com

- 1888PressRelease.com

- MarketWire.com

- BusinessWire.com

- PRLeap.com

- PRNewswire.com

- PR.com

- SBWire.com

Social Media
Connect and Click With Your Customers

Social media is a highly effective inbound marketing tool to create awareness about your product or service. Social media websites allow visitors to share and discuss ideas, experiences, photos, videos, and audio. In the early versions of the Internet, websites were one dimensional; they pushed information at the visitor and didn't allow for feedback or sharing information among visitors. Social media networks now encourage visitors to comment and share content. Today, social networking isn't relegated to social media websites; virtually all websites have a social element to them.

Social media has many business applications for home builders. First, we do business with people we like and trust, and social media allows builders to connect with prospective buyers and current/past owners on a more personal level. Social media gives your audience a controlled glimpse into your business. Second, social media works because customers trust other customers more than they trust you (the business). When one of your homeowners posts how much they love their new home or neighborhood, that is worth more than any form of paid advertising.

A 2012 Nielsen report[11] found that 92 percent of consumers trusted recommendations from friends and family more than they did any other form of advertising. Online consumer reviews were trusted by 70 percent of consumers. Other trusted sources include 58 percent of ads on brand websites, 50 percent of opt-in emails, 47 percent of TV ads, 47 percent of magazine ads, 46 percent of newspaper ads, and 42 percent of radio ads.

Finally, social media shapes consumer behavior. Consumers feel empowered by social media to have their voice heard, which can work for or against you. "According to a study by OTX Research, about two-thirds of customers use the information they find through social media to influence their buying decisions. More than 67 percent are also likely to pass this information on to others, and more than 60 percent trust information they find through social media more than traditional advertisements."[12]

Your prospective customers want to hear from other customers that you offer a great product, for a great price, with great customer service. It means so much more than anything you have to say. I've found that the ultimate online marketing formula is **Search + Social = Sales**. Your search engine marketing strategy helps buyers find you. Step two includes your social media networking presence, so customers can research what others say about your business and brand.

I mentioned earlier about our move from Florida to North Carolina. I used the Web heavily during the moving process. First, I used Google to search for businesses near my new home. Once I found several options, I reviewed their websites for information about services and pricing. Then I narrowed down the list to three to five businesses and browsed Facebook to further research each one. If I could find a Facebook Business Page with positive reviews and pictures, it made the cut to the final two much easier. If I couldn't find any reviews or recommendations, the business was cut from consideration. I also posted on my personal Facebook page, asking for recommendations. When several of the businesses I had already found through my search popped up from my friends on Facebook, the business went straight to the front of the line. Once I narrowed down the search to two local businesses, I visited them each in person. Social media for business is the equivalent of word of mouth on steroids.

Social media is not always a large traffic driver to your website. It can be, but it isn't a given like SEO or paid search marketing. Be very clear about your goals before you start or enhance your social media presence. The average social media post, whether it's text, a photo, or video isn't going to drive a lot of traffic. Visitors use social media sites to talk to their friends and interact with others. A handful may click on the link to your site, but most will see your post, hopefully click Like, or retweet and move on.

If you want social media to be a traffic driver, that will require a special promotion, coupon, or contest on the social media site supported by paid ads.

So why use it to market your business? Social media marketing is the new word-of-mouth marketing. It's that simple. You cannot afford to ignore the conversation that is happening online about your product category and/or your company. As a result, home builders are rapidly moving advertising dollars out of traditional media options and implementing social media marketing.

Popular social media networks:

- Facebook

- LinkedIn

- Twitter

- YouTube

- Instagram

- Pinterest

- Yelp

The Nuts and Bolts of Social Media

How Does It Work Exactly?

If you aren't actively participating on social media networks, they may feel a bit overwhelming to you. Social media is a vital asset to home builders and your online marketing strategy. You need to be a part of the online conversation happening—with or without you—on social networks. Here are the steps to begin setting up your social networks and joining the conversation with your fans.

Step #1 – Set up an account on the social media website of your choice.

Please note that Facebook specifically has several different account types, including a personal page, business page (also known as a fan page), company/organization/institution page, brand/product page, artist/band/public figure page, entertainment page, and a cause/community page. BEFORE you set up an account, you need to determine the purpose of your page in order to select the right page type. Keep in mind that once you name your page, you can only change it one time after you have more than twenty-five fans. Name your Facebook page with a title that will encompass current and future business endeavors. If the name you've chosen no longer applies to your business, you only have one opportunity to change it. If you want to change your Facebook page again, you have to start over with a new account and you can't automatically transfer your friends and fans to your new page.

Step #2 – Customize your page with copy and images.

Always fill out the profile completely for all of your social media networks. Describe your business in detail and include search engine keywords in the copy. Create a photo album for each available home, neighborhood, or floor plan. Add videos, homeowner testimonials, and links to other social websites. Integrate the content from your other social networks too. As you add more content to your page, you create a richer experience for your visitors, and they will be more likely to share your content with their friends and followers.

Step #3 – Build your connections.

Based on the information you enter into your profile, the social media website recommends other people you may know. You have the option to invite their recommendations to be your friends, followers, or connections. You can also search the website for people you know and/or you can upload your online address book and send an email invitation to connect through the social network. Once you become connected to another person on the website, you can see their friends and you can invite those friends to connect with you as well. It takes time to build an engaged, active community of friends and fans on your social media networks. Think of it as the online equivalent of in-person networking.

Step #4 – Interact frequently.

The goal of social networks is to post your own content and engage with your friends and fans. You may wonder why someone cares about what your business is doing on a daily basis, or if anyone would want to be a fan of your business. Human beings are hardwired to connect with each other and build relationships—particularly women. Social media allows you to build those connections online. With the click of the mouse, your fans can catch up with old friends, ask for referrals of a product or service, and network with other professionals. Human beings, by nature, are also curious and self-centered. Seriously.

For more information about social networking for business, I encourage you to pick up a copy of my newest book, *The Fan Factor*.[13] This book takes an in-depth view into the world of social networking and helps businesspeople understand why fans want to interact with your business in a more personal way. You will also discover how to produce engaging content your fans will love.

I also recommend Carol Morgan's, *Social Media for Home Builders 3.0: It's Easier Than You Think*.[14] Morgan's book is the home builder industry go-to guide for social media. It is packed with case studies and practical examples about how to implement a social marketing strategy. The book is available at BuilderBooks.com.

Does Social Media Work?

Yes. Absolutely.

Like Search Engine Optimization, you should begin your social media journey with the right expectations. Social media marketing takes time to mature and does not generally produce immediate results. Expect a social media campaign to take a minimum of six months to produce quality results. You have no time to waste. Get started already.

Social Media Tips:

- **Don't join all the social media networks at once.** Stick to a couple of networks that you intuitively enjoy and can update consistently.

- **Narrow down your networks to ones your target audience uses regularly.** Are you targeting consumers or other business people? Does your target audience prefer video or text? How often does your audience want to hear from you? What is your audience passionate about? If you target other business people, LinkedIn should be your main social networking site. If you target women, focus on Facebook. If you target young, tech-savvy professionals, start tweeting on Twitter.

- **Be consistent and efficient.** Social media requires a consistent effort. Plan to spend a few minutes a day interacting. Just like in-per-

son networking, half the battle is showing up. If someone emails you
or posts on your profile, respond immediately.

- **Use a smart phone to help manage the extra work social media requires.** If you have a smart phone, you can find those extra minutes to engage with your fans while on the go. It's easy to sneak in a quick post between meetings, waiting in line at the grocery store, or waiting for your child to finish soccer practice. A smart phone also helps you post more than text updates since you can snap a picture or film a video of a funny sign, happy customer, or a mundane observation (think Jerry Seinfeld). This will make your posts more interesting. Just please don't text, email, or post while driving.

- **Be clear and realistic about the results.** Social media is a long-term commitment. You won't sell a home the first day. Just like in-person networking, it takes time to develop your online relationships. Be patient and pay your dues.

- **Don't sell too hard.** If you're posting purely sales messages every day or multiple times a day, your connections will tune you out. Be clever, be fun, and incorporate a bit of your personal life. Social media is about pulling people toward you, not pushing advertising at them.

- **Beware of social media "netiquette."** That picture of you dancing on the table with a drink in your hand is FOREVER online once you post it. There is no clear line between your personal and professional life in social media. It all blends together. You can set certain filters on your profile, but it's better to be safe than sorry. NEVER, EVER, EVER post anything negative about your job, employer, immediate supervisor, product, or service. NEVER. Period. The end.

- **Give value that your audience will appreciate.** What is your audience passionate about? Deliver that information. You can post tips, facts, trivia, quotes, links, photos, videos, or anything your audience will find interesting. These posts may or may not be directly about your company or homes.

- **Plan for negative comments in advance.** Some builders feel the possibility of a negative comment is a reason to avoid social media. If someone is so upset with your company that they are willing to post something negative about you online, they will post it somewhere. Why not allow them to post it in a place where you can answer immediately. Have a service recovery plan in place if someone posts something negative about your company, homes, floor plans, neighborhoods, etc. It may not happen, but what if it does? Plan who will respond and what the message will be. Don't be caught off guard and too slow to answer.

- **Don't overexpose yourself.** I am not referring to the Alec Baldwin "laptop bedroom" scene in *It's Complicated*. You can overdo it on social media. There is no need for businesses to tweet every hour on the hour. It's annoying. A couple of tweets per day or updates on Facebook are plenty. Companies that post too many times a day look like they aren't busy and have time to play around. That's the opposite of what you are trying to achieve. With your iPhone firmly placed in your left hand, raise your right hand and repeat after me: "I do solemnly swear to stop overexposing myself on social media." With so many individuals and businesses using social media to connect with their customers, the sheer volume of posts is almost unmanageable. From Mafia Wars to Farmville, I am hiding applications and friends with reckless abandon. I suspect I am not alone. Overexposure on social media means you are either posting too often, posting annoying material, and/or selling too hard.

- **Post with purpose.** Social media can be a total time sucker if you aren't focused and clear on your goal and purpose. It's easy to log in to post one link and two hours later still be clicking around. Know in advance what you are going to post and stick to it.

How do you begin your social media journey?

1. If possible, appoint a dedicated social media ambassador for your company. This person's responsibility is to either update all social media on behalf of your company and/or manage an outside social media firm. You can't stop your employees from posting about you, but your ambassador can monitor what is posted and alert you quickly if any problems arise.

2. Set up accounts. Have a master list of all your social media network usernames and passwords. Make sure the accounts aren't linked to anyone's personal account at the company. You want complete control of these accounts. If an outside firm sets up accounts for you, have them give you the usernames and passwords so you can access them if you terminate their services.

3. Write down your goals. What do you want to achieve from social media? Be realistic. Are you hoping to generate leads, brand awareness, or improve SEO? How will you know if your efforts are working? (Hint … Google Analytics.)

4. Review your website analytics report. Determine a baseline of your current traffic numbers and sources before you start any new social media campaign. Review your numbers each month or before and after specific campaigns. Discuss what works and what you can improve each month.

5. Plan each month's postings and tweets in advance. What do you want to tell the online world about your company, homes, neighborhoods, and floor plans? Brainstorm ways to add value to your posts.

6. Start building your connections. Spend time combing through your connections and those of your friends and fans. Build as many connections as you can each month.

7. Coordinate your social messages with your other marketing efforts. You should cross-promote any traditional marketing efforts in your social media networks.

8. Be patient. It takes time and energy to grow your online fan base. Work in your accounts every day or stay in touch with your social media firm to keep them diligent. Social media requires consistency and repetition to be effective.

You know you are a social media flasher (overexposing) when you:

1. Post too often. How often is too often? How often you post on your social media networks depends on the quality of your posts and your target audience. Keep your posts educational, informational, thoughtful, or humorous. In the era of social media, spam isn't limited to email. You can spam your friends, fans, and followers by posting more than a couple of times a day.

If you are a self-employed business person, over-posting can make others wonder how busy you are with paying customers. Posting too frequently may come across desperate and a little too eager. One of my favorite posting mistakes is what I call machine gun posting—the act of posting more than one post at a time. If you are simultaneously posting five different promotional videos to sell your latest home, stop the madness. We heard you the first time.

2. Post annoying material. This is another highly subjective topic. Content that is annoying to some is highly entertaining to others. I love to post about the Florida Gators and find Florida State Seminole posts highly annoying. I'm sure most people with good taste would agree, but a few of you out there might feel differently. (Although I can't imagine why.) While it's hard to quantify what is an annoying post, you know one when you see it. A truly annoying post is one that comes across as disingenuous. Great posts are authentic and representative of the person or business. Great posts are clever, sometimes humorous, and more about the audience than about you. Post what your audience needs, wants, or cares about and you can't go wrong.

3. Sell too hard. This is easy to quantify. If you post more than one sales message a day, you are selling too hard. The best practice is a five-to-one ratio. Post five educational, informational, and/or personal posts to one sales post. Remember, this is called *social* media, not *sales* media.

People want to connect, communicate, and collaborate. Keep it personal and fun.

Mix in some appropriate personal content with your posts. We want to see your kid's Christmas pageant photo (but just one or two please). We want to know that your husband won yard of the month. We love your pet photos, funny website links, and Seinfeld-esque observational humor. We like getting to know you on a personal level. **People do business with people they like and trust.** Take note of that sentence. It doesn't read: *People do business with fan pages that have lots of shopping cart links.*

When you use social media, think of it as an in-person networking event. In-person networking etiquette says to work through the room, shake hands, and smile. Build rapport. Ask more about the other person than you talk about yourself. Wear your name tag and give out plenty of cards, but don't go for the hard close the first time you meet someone. Be memorable and, above all, be yourself.

Content Marketing
The Heart of your Social Media Strategy

Content marketing is the creation of value-added information about your product or service to attract prospects. One of the most effective content marketing tools is a blog. Blogging is no longer reserved for activists, political junkies, and struggling writers. Today, blogging is a mainstream Web marketing activity used by many organizations to expand their online presence.

There are two main reasons why home builders should blog. The first reason is that blogging improves your website's organic search engine positioning. Search engines love blog posts. They usually rank them higher than the homepage of your website. This increases your chance of a page one ranking. Search engines love websites with fresh content. Consistent blogging each month will add new pages to your website with fresh content on a regular basis.

A blog also acts as a hub for your social media marketing (reason number two). Social media sites come and go and frequently change posting visibility rules. These constant changes limit your ability to control the campaign and its effectiveness. When you create a social media profile on a site like Facebook, you are building a presence on rented land. What happens if Facebook or any of the social sites go the way of MySpace? A better practice is to build a social hub on land you own, a self-hosted blog.

A blog also allows you to explore topics more in-depth and include visuals such as photos and videos. **Think of your blog as the library or repository for your content and the social media networks, like Facebook, as drivers who direct traffic to the hub.**

Creating a blog will also give potential buyers a chance to interact with you in a different format and build brand awareness.

Factors to Consider Before You Begin Blogging

1. Who will write the content and maintain the blog?

You have two options: 1) Manage and write the blog in-house or 2) Out-source part or all of the posts. If you outsource the content creation and/or blog management, you will still have to provide the blogger with the core content. No one knows your business and your target audience as well as you do. Think carefully about which person in your organization can focus the time and energy necessary to provide the blogger with core content on a consistent basis.

2. Will you use a free template blog or a paid customized blog?

We build all new websites with an integrated custom blog. If you have an older website and you are not ready to invest in a new one, you can set up a blog on a free platform like Blogger.com or Wordpress.com. Sign up for an account and use the fairly easy online editors to customize the template with your company logo, photos, or other graphics.

For best results, hire a professional web designer to design a customized blog to match your current marketing materials and integrate into your current website. The back-end of the blog can be either a proprietary blog platform or you can use an open source platform, like the paid version of Wordpress (found at Wordpress.org).

Which one is right for you? The answer lies in your budget and level of commitment. If you see blogging as a vital part of your long-term Web marketing strategy, then make the up-front investment in the paid cus-tomized route.

Some home builders find the idea of writing a blog for their company daunting because they don't know how or where to come up with con-tent. The good news is you don't have to write the great American novel to write an effective blog post. A post of around 300 words is the ideal length. Don't underestimate the value of quick tips, check lists, and bullet points in your posts. Readers love something they can scan quickly for "aha" ideas.

Writing a blog post is not as hard as you may think. In fact, I'm going to share with you ten ideas to jump-start your thought process so you can share useful information with your target audience.

1. List helpful how-to tips related to your products.

2. Explain why you are so passionate about your business or your community.

3. Describe a day in the life of your business or behind-the-scenes tidbits of your daily routine.

4. Review other home builder industry/consumer blogs.

5. Go to a trade fair or conference and write reports about it.

6. Answer FAQs from your customers.

7. Describe your customer service philosophy.

8. Make a list of must-have free resources your audience will appreciate.

9. Sign up for Google Alerts on home builder topics and then blog about related news stories.

10. Run a contest, offering a free product sample or service for the winner. Then ask the winner to comment about their experience.

Include a call to action at the end of your blog post. You could ask for reader comments or encourage your readers to visit your website. Spread the word about your blog on your other social networks. Remember, the more often you publish useful content for your readers, the more likely they'll come to rely on you as a trusted source, which will convert your readers into leads for your business.

How to Write a Blog Post That Rocks

Now that you've built the blog and decided who will write the posts, it's time to begin. If you haven't blogged before, or if you want to enhance your posts, these tips will help.

1. **Think outside the blog.** All blog posts should not be about your company and product. Your goal should be to provide interesting/helpful information about your business/home builder industry and interesting stories to attract visitors to your blog for additional information. To determine what content will engage your readers, create a profile of your last ten home buyers. Where do they eat, shop, and work? What kind of cars do they drive? What is their favorite thing to do on the weekend? Once you compile a profile, relate your typical buyer's lifestyle to your homes. Good blog posts showcase how your homes enhance the buyer's lifestyle by helping them save money, stay organized, get into shape, and spend more time with family and friends. Speak to the heart of your readers and you will have very engaging content.

2. **Don't be so formal**. Have fun. If you live in an area with plenty of local flavor, take pictures and film short videos of people enjoying the lifestyle. Post the photos or video and write a few sentences to summarize the event. Don't forget to work-in your search engine keywords.

3. **Keep it conversational.** Have you ever read a blog post that was more like an instructional manual? Don't lose your visitors by talking *at* them. An easy way to begin a post is to brainstorm a list of questions your prospective buyers frequently ask. Write one blog post to answer each question on the list. If you write as if you are speaking out loud and answering someone's question, you will write in a more conversational tone.

4. **Encourage interaction.** Invite visitors to post comments on each story. Ask for their suggestions and personal experiences. Consider run-

ning a fun contest to encourage visitors to post their favorite picture or video (rated G of course) of them moving into their new home or enjoying your community amenities. You can also offer giveaways and incentives to those who post and interact in a positive way.

For some businesses, the fear of negative comments keeps them from starting a blog. If a customer is so angry about a perceived lack of service or product defect, you can bet they will post that frustration somewhere online. Why not allow them to post where you can monitor, respond, and recover? If they post those feelings somewhere else, you have no chance to respond. If you are absolutely against allowing negative comments, you can set up your blog to moderate and block them.

5. **Link up**. Make sure your blog links to your homepage, social media networks, and other industry websites that provide additional information for your visitor. Ask other websites to include links to your website to create ongoing reciprocating links. Just like you build traffic to your corporate website, you build traffic to your blog. Whenever you post a new blog, post notices on Facebook, LinkedIn, Twitter, and other social media networks to alert your friends, fans, and followers.

6. **Don't reinvent the wheel.** Occasionally, you can blog about another blog. For example, if you see a great blog post about the industry, it's okay to post about that blog as long as full credit is given to the author and you link back to their blog. Never copy another blogger's material without giving full credit and a link. Do not plagiarize content posted on your blog. You would not appreciate another blogger copying your original content, so don't do it to others. It is never okay to re-blog content from a paid membership website. If the website is charging members to read the content, the publisher won't appreciate you giving it away for free

7. **Don't always sell, sell, sell.** A blog should not be a glorified sales pitch. Constant selling turns visitors off your blog and social media. Blogs are meant to inform, educate, and entertain. Of course, you can mix in some self-promotion, but a blog should not sell your products all the time.

Nobody likes to read pushy sales copy constantly.

8. Include images and other media. You've probably heard the expression, "content is king." It's true that great copy essentially hooks your reader. Images also play an important role on your blog. As you write your posts, think about what images would enhance the copy and bring it to life visually. Logos, product images, lifestyle photos, author photo, infographics, and event photos make great visuals. Videos are even more compelling than still images. Anytime you can include a short video with your post, go for it.

9. Encourage social sharing. If you want to grow the audience for your business blog, keep your content in front of your readers. That means posting links to your articles on social networks like Facebook, Twitter, Google+, and LinkedIn. Include social share bars or icons, like the Google +1 button. Don't forget to ask readers to share your blog with a call to action. Dan Zarella of Hubspot found Twitter users are up to four times more likely to retweet when asked to do so.[15]

10. Invite guest bloggers. Don't rely solely on your employees (or yourself) as the main contributor to your blog. Ask outside experts to write articles. Their participation will add enormous credibility to your blog and provide an implied endorsement of your company.

How Do You Know if Your Blog Works?

The beauty of Web marketing lies in easily tracking and measuring results. If you have a free template blog, the platform generally provides free basic-level tracking. You can monitor the number of visitors, websites referring traffic to your blog, and which posts are most popular. If you have a paid, customized blog, you can install more advanced tracking, like Google Analytics, to provide an in-depth review of the blog's performance. Review your reports on a monthly basis and adjust as necessary.

There is an art and science to blogging. The blogosphere has its own language and culture. The best way to begin your journey is to subscribe to several of your favorite blogs to watch and learn appropriate behaviors. Once you monitor them for a while, the next step is to start posting comments. After you become comfortable posting comments and interacting, you are ready to begin strategizing who will manage your own blog, what type of blog you need, and what content you will blog about. Once you start, don't stop. Post consistently, don't sell too hard, and have fun. Entering the blogosphere is an incredibly educational and worthwhile ride.

What to Look for In a Social Media Consultant/Firm

Like SEO, there are many social media marketing firms out there. It is a very hot topic. Just because someone dabbles in social media for their own business doesn't make them an expert. You need a *real* social media expert. Look for a firm that specializes in social media and understands the true essence of this burgeoning online activity. Ask for case studies and references. Also look for someone who has a strong marketing background. Any technical person knows how to push buttons. Experienced marketers know how to plan your message, coordinate your online and offline marketing, and brainstorm clever ways to add value online.

Online Marketing Overload

WHEW! Now that you've read about all of your online marketing options, are you TOTALLY overwhelmed? That's okay. The next section will help you narrow down your options. The best way to determine what will work best is to ask a lot of questions about the purpose, goal, and desired outcome of your marketing strategy.

First, determine if you need a long-term strategy or a short-term strategy to push a particular neighborhood, available home, or home site. A long-term strategy uses different online marketing tools than a short-term campaign. Many builders only focus on the short-term and experience peaks and valleys in sales. If you think bigger picture and more long-term strategy, you will save marketing dollars and experience even more sales results.

Questions to ask about your online marketing strategy:

1. What is the overall marketing goal of your company and what role will marketing play?

2. What is your annual marketing budget? What portion of the budget can be devoted to online marketing?

3. What traditional marketing line items can be eliminated to add dollars for more online marketing?

4. What offline marketing options are you considering? Do they have a proven track record of success?

5. What online marketing options are you considering? Have they worked for you in the past? Why or why not?

6. Do you need a long-term strategy to position your company in the

market, or a short-term strategy to drive immediate results? Do you need both?

7. Who will oversee the Web marketing?

8. What is your online marketing sophistication level?

9. Is a compelling website already in place? How up-to-date is the website? How many leads per month does it average?

10. Is there an online lead follow-up process in place to maximize return on investment?

11. What are your sales goals?

12. Does a CRM (Customer Relationship Management) system manage the permission email list?

13. Do you have Google Analytics embedded on your website to track marketing results?

14. Are the sales people properly trained on how to convert online leads into sales with effective follow-up, demonstration, and closing skills?

15. How often will you meet to review online marketing results?

16. How will you evaluate the success of online marketing campaigns?

17. What online marketing tactics are your competitors using?

18. What content do you already have (photos, videos, articles) that can be leveraged to streamline your workload?

19. What portion of the online marketing can be outsourced?

20. Who is the final decision maker and who will implement your online marketing plan?

Certain components are more effective than others, depending on the answers to these questions.

Short-term solutions with immediate impact, excellent for lead generation, moving inventory, and special offers/promotions include:

- Paid search (PPC)

- Online display advertising

- Behavioral targeting banners

- Referral websites

- Email marketing

- Social media contests

- Special promotions/campaigns

- Event marketing

Long-term solutions excellent for building brand awareness and interest include:

- Search engine optimization (SEO)

- Social media networks

- Blogging

- Online public relations

- Free listing websites

- Content marketing

If you consider your marketing goal, timing, budget, audience, and offline media, you can confidently select the right online marketing components for your specific marketing needs.

How do you begin?

1. Identify and profile your target market.

2. Invest in the best website (hub) you can afford.

3. Select at least two to three traffic drivers.

4. Write down the promotions and the timing.

5. Measure and track the first promotion.

6. Adjust where needed.

7. Rinse and repeat.

CHAPTER 5

Building Block #3
Online Lead Follow-Up

It's five o'clock; do you know where your online leads are?

Now that you have a WOW website and a diverse marketing mix driving traffic, how do you plan to manage and convert your visitors into sales? The Click Power Strategy means nothing if you don't generate new sales from your efforts.

Once you implement the first two building blocks in the strategy, the number of online leads you receive will increase. You need a process to turn these leads into sales. Winging it won't work.

Many business owners have no idea what happens to the online leads that come from their website. Following up on online requests will give you a competitive advantage. Most home builders do not have a follow-up plan for this type of lead.

I am so passionate about follow-up. Before starting my own business, I sold online advertising to home builders for Move.com. I eventually realized my clients had no idea what to do with the leads we were producing. I also realized I needed to teach them what to do quickly or I would have a short career. I began offering free seminars about how to manage Web leads to sell more advertising.

Unfortunately, or fortunately as it turned out, audiences were less interested in buying more Move.com advertising since they were hiring me to speak/consult for their company. Seminar participants would greet me after these free programs and ask me what I would charge to speak at their company. At that time my answer was, "What would you pay?" Now I am ready with an answer.

The car industry is a shining example of how to transform online information requests into sales. Most car dealers have a dedicated online salesperson that fields the website requests, follows up on them, and converts them into sales. The online salesperson is fast, efficient, and customer service oriented. Online salespeople usually receive the best ratings in the dealership because they provide such an awesome service to their customers. Look to the car industry for ideas about how to follow-up on your own website leads and convert them into sales.

As a home builder, you have to deal with the issue of digital communication and how your company will handle it. You can't afford to be unresponsive, especially in the age of Twitter where it is too easy to tweet customer service frustrations. If you are still unsure if a dedicated online sales person is right for your company, consider the following:

- With the right person and processes in place, centralized online sales programs work BIG TIME. I have monitored dozens of these sales programs and they consistently **contribute 30+ percent of total sales** (some contribute more than 40 percent).

- It is possible to quantify and benchmark the results of your online sales program.

- Appointments drive sales. If you want to convert online leads to sales, set more appointments. Appointments are the number one determinant of your online sales program's success.

- Email marketing follow-up works best when it's personalized and highly targeted. Consumers are tired of the "blast and bury" email marketing approach. Get personal to get their attention.

- Relying on New Home Consultants (onsite agents) to follow-up with online leads doesn't work. Onsite agents don't have the time or tools to follow-up properly.

Read this chapter with an open mind and start brainstorming how you can take this information and apply it to your business model today.

1. The speed of your first reply

How fast are you? Most companies aren't fast enough. In March 2011, *Harvard Business Review*[16] audited the response time to web-generated test leads of 2,241 U.S. companies. The study found 24 percent took more than twenty-four hours and 23 percent never responded at all. The average response time was forty-two hours.

The most telling outcome of the study was this: "Firms that tried to contact potential customers within an hour of receiving a query were nearly seven times as likely to qualify the lead (which we defined as having a meaningful conversation with a key decision maker) as those that tried to contact the customer even an hour later—and more than sixty times as likely as companies that waited twenty-four hours or longer."

SmartTouch Interactive, a leading home builder CRM (Customer Relationship Management) software company, reports that out of 425 new home communities shopped, 53 percent did not follow-up with the buyer, 23 percent followed-up in seventy-two hours, and 18 percent in twenty-four hours.

If you want to convert more online leads to sales, you need a fast response. I am often asked if an email auto responder will suffice (this is an automatic email response from your website sent immediately after a visitor submits a request). Auto responders buy you time, but they mostly acknowledge that the request was received. They do little to build a relationship and nurture the prospect into a sale. Once the response is sent, the clock is ticking to deliver a more personalized reply with specific answers to the inquiry.

A National Association of Realtors 2009 study discovered that 20 percent of consumers expect an immediate response from a real estate agent and 19 percent expect a thirty-minute response. They also found that the chances of reaching an online lead are 100 percent if you respond within ten minutes compared to 50 percent within twenty-four hours.[17]

Think of an online lead as the digital equivalent of someone holding out his or her hand for a handshake. By failing to respond, or responding slowly, you are refusing to shake their hand. Your follow-up cannot be too fast, it can only be too slow.

2. The number of times you follow-up

Sending out one email response is not enough. From my experience of monitoring online leads, you can follow up via email up to six times (if the prospect does not respond) before the prospect is ready to blow up your computer. For every online lead, you should send out up to six personalized email responses. Once you engage the online lead in a conversation, discontinue the automated response and converse as the situation warrants.

3. Your email copy

If your email lacks compelling copy, you won't get results. First, you need to determine the goal of the email. Are you trying to set an appointment, find out the prospect's phone number, or generate walk-in traffic? You should only have one goal per email. An email that tries to do too much is confusing to the consumer.

Keep your email copy short and use bulleted lists whenever possible. Consumers don't read email, they scan it. Write short paragraphs and get to the point fast.

4. The quantity and quality of your online leads

Is the right target market visiting your website? Are you receiving enough online leads to your website? Just like with traditional marketing, the more targeted the traffic, the higher the conversion rate. To properly judge the quality of your online leads, you should first track the lead source and then track the outcome.

5. Your product, price, and/or location

The quality, price, and/or location of your product will directly impact how many online lead registrations you receive. No marketing magic will fix this type of problem. Many home builders demand to know why their online efforts are not more successful, and I hate pointing out that the product, price, or location is less than desirable to their target market.

6. The offline experience

It's not enough to deliver a WOW online experience. The offline experience has to match the quality of the online experience, or it will hurt your conversion rate. Remember to keep a smooth transition from online to offline and a pleasant, knowledgeable, friendly person waiting to assist your customer in the offline world.

What Is Your Online Lead Follow-Up Process?

Since you can't react too quickly when following up with your prospects and you need repeated, personalized messages to reach your customers, your best option is to dedicate a staff member to manage your Web leads. For the purposes of this book, I refer to this position as an Online Sales Counselor (OSC).

Depending on the size of your company, you may not need a full-time person to field your Web leads. You may want to give this responsibility to someone on your team who is tech savvy, friendly, knowledgeable about your products, and likes to talk to people. This is by no means the ideal situation, but it can work. Ideally, hire someone full-time to respond and follow up.

How do you know what approach is right for you? The volume of on-line requests will answer that question. If you only receive a couple of requests per week from your website, then the builder or sales manager can personally manage the follow-up effectively. Once you reach more than fifteen to twenty-five requests per week, hire someone to manage the requests for you in a timely manner.

View the OSC role as a salesperson in disguise as a customer service representative. On the surface, the OSC is helpful, friendly, and non-threatening, but is actually working with each lead to build a relationship that will eventually result in an offline visit and sale.

The Online Sales Counselor (OSC) Position

1. What exactly will the OSC do?

- Give an instant, personalized response to all online leads.

- Follow up with an online lead until he/she either sets an appointment or asks to be removed from your email list.

- Hand off online leads to the onsite sales counselor when he/she sets an onsite appointment.

- Follow up with the online lead after the appointment.

- Maintain the company's website.

- Maintain the CRM (Customer Relationship Management) software.

- Continually update online lead records with notes and comments from customers.

- Track the online lead to sale conversion rate.

- Answer a toll-free hotline.

- Manage and maintain the Live Chat service on your website.

- Develop new email marketing campaigns.

- Build and maintain relationships with outside real estate agents.

2. How far will the OSC go into the sales process?

- This varies based on your business model. It is better to implement part of this program and ensure a faster response than not at all. If you can't hire a full-time OSC, perhaps one of your agents would take on additional responsibility to manage online leads.

- The most successful model, from my experience, allows the OSC to serve as an appointment-setting service, effectively moving the online lead from online to offline. Once the prospect arrives at the offline location, a sales agent takes over the process.

3. How many online leads can one OSC manage?

- A good rule of thumb is 250 online leads per month. This number is only possible if you have an efficient email marketing database that automates the follow-up process. If you receive more than 250 leads per month, you will need multiple OSCs.

4. How will we compensate the OSC?

- Compensation varies based on your business model. Some OSCs make a base salary with a bonus structure, while others work on straight commission.

- Base salary should be equivalent to an administrative assistant or sales assistant.

- Bonus structure should depend on the experience of the OSC. "Appointments kept" bonus amounts start at $25/appointment for beginners and go up. "Sales" (sales generated from kept appointments) bonus amounts start at $250/sale for beginners and go up. There are many experienced OSCs making six figures, which is very positive for the builder because the number is tied to performance.

- Make sure part of the compensation is tied to performance—either by number of appointments set and kept and/or number of sales from those appointments.

5. What hours will the OSC work?

- Good OSCs never ask this question. They will respond day or night on their smartphone if it means making a conversion.

6. Will we take the OSC's bonus out of the offline sales person's commission?

- Please don't penalize the offline sales team and take part of their commission away. **This will kill the program.** You want the entire sales department working together as a team—not feeling threatened by each other.

7. What can I expect from the OSC?

- Expect to see some appointments set and kept within ninety days of beginning the program. Your OSC should generate sales within six months.

Tools of the Trade

Now that you have defined the parameters of the program, it's time to think about the tools and resources needed for the success of the program.

Your OSC will need the following:

- Workspace in your office. Your OSC can work from home, but it requires a VERY self-motivated and highly-disciplined person to make this work. It's best if you allocate quiet office space so the OSC can talk on the phone in a professional environment.

- FAST laptop computer with a high-speed Internet connection (and wireless connection).

- Dedicated business line. I know with the pervasive use of cell phones that landlines seem dated, but offering a toll-free number makes you appear very customer service oriented. This is more about positioning yourself than practical use.

- Wi-Fi enabled smartphone and/or tablet, preferably an Apple or Android product since a large number of apps are available on these devices. A smartphone will help your OSC respond quickly on the go.

- Collateral material, including brochures, postcards, letters, and DVDs to mail to online leads requesting printed information.

- CRM (Customer Relationship Management) database.

- Series of personalized email auto-response letters.

- Email marketing templates.

- Live Chat service.

- Training on setting up the CRM system, follow-up processes, closing for appointments, and email marketing.

Hiring the Right Online Sales Counselor (OSC)

If you want a centralized online sales program to work, then you need to hire the RIGHT person for the OSC position.

What kind of person are you looking for?

- **Database experience** – This person must have an intuitive knowledge of how databases function, including how to enter contact records, sort records, categorize records into targeted lists, and pull custom reports.

- **Computer literate** – Including Microsoft Office programs such as Word, Excel, and Access.

- **Graphic design abilities** – Knowledge of Photoshop and Illustrator is extremely helpful. We live in a visual communication society, so photo and graphic editing skills are necessary.

- **Web savvy** – Ask the candidate if they shop online and, if so, what they shop for? If he/she orders products and services online, there is a good chance he/she has an understanding of the expectations and demands of today's digital customer.

- **Professional writing skills** – Since he/she will correspond heavily via email, ask to see a sample email and rate how professionally he/she writes.

- **Highly organized** – Ask for specific examples in the interview.

- **Telephone skills** – Your OSC must love talking on the telephone. Someone with good phone skills is ideal. This person should not lack sales skills. Remember, the most important part of the job is appointment setting, which happens primarily on the phone.

- **Creative and innovative** – He/she should always think outside the box and look for new technology solutions to keep you ahead of the curve.

- **Passionate about sales and marketing** – This is a crossover position that requires both sales and marketing skills.

- **Someone who loves people** – Ask for specific examples in a retail environment.

- **Hungry to succeed** – A great OSC is motivated and energized by bonuses and commission compensation plans.

Where do you find this person?

- Look at your existing staff members first. Often, an offline salesperson, who is tech savvy, would love to take on a new role at your company. The online sales program will produce results much more quickly with an existing staff member who already knows your products and company.

- If you don't have any internal candidates, post the available position on websites such as Careerbuilder.com, Monster.com, and Hotjobs.com. You are looking for people who use the Web to seek information.

- Describe the position as an inside sales position. Screen resumes for people who have a background using the telephone and a database.

Online Sales Counselor - Sample Job Description

Company: ABC Homes

Location: Orlando, FL

Status: Full-Time Employee

Job Description:

ABC Homes is currently seeking an Online Sales Counselor (OSC) who will support our online sales and marketing initiatives. The position responds, qualifies, and manages online lead information requests. The individual will report directly to the Sales and Marketing Manager.

Job Responsibilities:

- Provide same day, immediate email/phone response to all online leads.

- Qualify online leads and follow-up accordingly.

- Follow-up multiple times with online prospects until an appointment is made to meet with an offline salesperson.

- Send out marketing collateral to online leads.

- Maintain a database of online leads.

- Maintain a toll-free number and voicemail for online leads.

- Assist prospects in selecting the best product/service for them.

- Conduct and manage ongoing email campaigns, newsletters, and community launches.

- Provide reports of online lead activity and sales conve

- Perform customer surveys, aggregate data, and make tions based on results to improve the online customer experience.

- Perform and maintain competitive email marketing and Web market research.

- Other projects as assigned.

Job Qualifications:

- Enjoy sales and marketing activities.

- High energy, positive can-do attitude.

- Minimum Associate's Degree (Bachelor's Degree preferred) in marketing or related business field.

- Two years sales/marketing experience.

- Advanced Web, email, and sales contact database experience.

- Strong computer skills, including Microsoft Office and spreadsheet applications.

- Detail oriented, customer-focused follow-up skills.

- Excellent email writing and telephone communication skills.

- Solid organizational, planning, and managing skills.

- Works well in an unstructured environment, and can quickly tackle ad-hoc projects with minimal supervision.

- Experience working under deadlines.

What Makes an Online Sales Counselor WOW?

Remember the classic scene in the *Wizard of Oz* when Toto pulled back the curtain to reveal the *real* wizard? In the movie, the wizard was an ordinary person with an amazing machine that made munchkins, scarecrows, and lions shake in their boots.

In the world of online sales and marketing, the opposite is true. Ultimately, converting online leads into sales is not about technology—although it is very important to have a solid website as your foundation. It's about the extraordinary people behind the technology.

Many industries, including home building, find that a dedicated OSC is the BEST way to respond quickly, follow up, and manage Web leads. In short, the OSC's job is to build a virtual relationship with each and every online lead, one email, phone call, or Live Chat at a time. The OSC's magnetic personality, disciplined follow-up, and stellar communication skills engage and delight the online customer, which results in new sales.

OSCs are a growing community of sales professionals, and many are among the best salespeople in our industry. Well-honed online sales and marketing programs often produce as much as 30 percent of total sales each month. The purpose of this section is to "pull back the curtain" and answer one central question—what makes an Online Sales Counselor WOW?

WOW Factor #1—Passion for Online Sales

There is no substitute for passion. It transcends all other success factors. Quite simply, an effective OSC lives, breathes, and loves helping people. Unlike traditional salespeople, the OSC is particularly passionate about using technology to help others. From the geekier aspects of learning new technology, like Click-to-Call and Live Chat, to the time-honored fundamentals of relationship building, OSCs wouldn't change how or what they do for anything in the world.

I asked Claudine Koh, the OSC for Standard Pacific Homes in Tampa, FL, about the number one contributing factor to her success and she immediately replied via email, "I LOVE what I do!" I've seen this same enthusiasm around the country. These professionals are a unique breed of salespeople; they don't require the face-to-face interaction or the instant gratification of a quick sale to feel fulfilled and productive. They are patient and dedicated to finding the ultimate win–win solution for the online customer no matter how long that takes.

WOW Factor #2—Instant Response to Inquiries

Great OSCs are fast. In the time it takes you to read this section, Tanya Smith, the Internet Sales Manager for Landon Homes in Plano, TX, has already responded to several new leads, chatted with a couple of website visitors, and returned a phone call. Tanya talks fast, types fast, and thinks fast. When asked about her success, Tanya said, "I try to always be available to incoming leads and respond personally within a very short time frame. I want them to know I care."

How fast are you? If you rely on onsite agents to respond in between phone calls and appointments, you aren't fast enough. By the time your onsite agent finally sits down to open email, Tanya has already booked an onsite appointment with a lead and is halfway to closing the sale. You can't be too fast. You can only be too slow when it comes to online leads.

WOW Factor #3—Focused on Details

There is much to do each day in the Online Sales Department, including fielding online leads, hotline calls, sending out requested collateral marketing, creating and sending e-blasts, and administering the CRM system. You must have a concise plan to efficiently gather all discovery information and schedule an appointment onsite during one phone call.

The OSC is the ultimate multitasker. Top performers drop everything to respond quickly AND they also keep track of important details for the CRM (Customer Relationship Management) database. It's easy to become sidetracked when the phone is ringing, email is coming in, and follow-up tasks are piling up. Staying focused and having a plan is critical to ongoing success.

WOW Factor #4—Consistently Ask For the Appointment

The core responsibility of the OSC is to set appointments for online leads to visit the community, available home, or home site in person. Most prospective homebuyers won't buy until they kick the dirt. However, most online customers tend to stay super-glued to their chair, which makes setting in-person appointments challenging. Successful OSCs know how to move prospects from a desk chair to the model home by simply asking when the prospect can come out for a visit.

Appointments are the best way to convert your online leads to onsite sales. Consistently asking your online leads to visit your community or model home is the best way to improve your appointment-setting percentage. It never hurts to ask, right?

Many other factors are important to finding the right OSC, including disciplined ongoing follow-up and great communication skills. If you currently do not have an OSC, you have the flexibility to custom design a position to fit your business model. The key is to figure out how to maximize your Web leads and convert them into sales. Online sales programs take time to mature. There is no better time than right now to focus on your online sales and marketing. Follow the yellow brick road to more sales today. You need a wizard of the Web selling for you.

POST-IT Notes® No More!

If you aren't familiar with the term CRM, it stands for Customer Relationship Management. CRM software helps manage your contacts. It is an electronic rolodex. Since your CRM is a digital database, the data can be sorted and manipulated to produce subset lists.

Think of CRM as using the right tool for the job. What happens when you try to use a Phillips-head screwdriver on a flat-head screw? Nothing. If you try to manage your online leads with Post-It Notes® and shoe boxes, nothing will happen. You are using the wrong tools for the job.

Commonly used CRM programs include (alphabetical order):

- Access
- ACT
- BuildTopia
- Builder 1440
- Builders Copilot
- Constellation
- Infusionsoft
- iTracMedia
- Lasso
- Open Leads
- Outlook
- Pivotal
- Salesforce

- Sales Simplicity

- SmartTouch CRM

- Top Producer

Which CRM is right for you? That's like asking which air filter goes in your car without knowing the make and model of your car. **A CRM has a very specific fit to your organization.** The best way to figure out which program is best for your company is to request a demo from all the providers and compare pricing, benefits, and features.

Benefits of a CRM Program

There are four major benefits to using a CRM program:

1. A CRM automatically imports online leads.

2. A CRM automatically responds to online leads.

3. A CRM tracks conversion rates and media sources.

4. A CRM tracks email open rates, bounce-back rates, and click-through rates.

Benefit #1—Automatically Imports Online Leads

One major benefit of an email marketing database is the ability to automatically import online leads from your website. Think about how much time automatic imports would save when following up with your online customers. The automatic import feature works like a funnel. Consumers who register on your website are automatically funneled into the database. Most databases also funnel in online leads from third-party referral websites. Instead of online leads cluttering your inbox, they are automatically entered into the database. You can log on to the database multiple times throughout the day and your online leads are waiting for your reply.

Benefit #2—Automatically Responds to Online Leads

The second time-saving benefit of a CRM database is the automatic re-sponse of email follow-up letters to each lead on a set schedule. The best systems allow you to determine the schedule. This is called Email Drip Campaigns. I will cover how to write effective auto responder emails later in the book. For now, please note I am not talking about writing stuffy, form-letter-type auto responders. They will not work. But it is possible to write effective auto responders that give you the best of both worlds—automated response, which ensures consistency, and effectively-written messages that elicit a response.

Auto response schedule:

- Email #1—Instant auto response. Please note you should also send a personalized follow-up email within minutes. If a phone number is provided, call rather than email.

- Email #2—Auto response three days after inquiry.

- Email #3—Auto response seven days after inquiry.

- Email #4—Auto response fourteen days after inquiry.

- Email #5—Auto response twenty-one days after inquiry.

- Email #6—Auto response twenty-eight days after inquiry.

When a prospect responds to your emails, you should remove him/her from the automatic schedule, so he/she will not continue receiving ge-neric emails.

Most email marketing databases will also send either text-based email or HTML-based email. Text-based email only contains text. HTML con-tains graphics, including the company logo, photos, and hyperlinks. Very few traditional systems are equipped to send HTML email, which is gen-erally more effective.

The larger the volume of online leads, the more important this feature becomes. **VERY IMPORTANT: I would not invest in an email marketing database for the Online Sales Counselor without the pre-scheduled automatic response functionality.**

Benefit #3—Track Conversion Rates and Media Sources

If you really want to gauge the effectiveness of your online lead program, you need a database that tracks online leads from prospect to buyer. Your system will track which media sources generated the most online leads and which generated the most sales. This information is invaluable to your marketing budget.

Benefit #4—Track Email Open Rates, Bounce-Back Rates, and Click-Through Rates

If a tree falls in the forest and no one is around to hear it, did it really fall? If an email is sent out and no one is around to answer it, was it really opened?

By tracking the open rate (how many people opened the email), the bounce-back rate (how many emails were not delivered because of errors), and the click-through rate (how many people clicked on a link in the email and visited your website), you know exactly how well your email campaign performed. This is critical information.

Questions to Ask

The following is a list of questions to determine which CRM system is right for your company.

1. Is the system software-based or Web-based?

If only one person will use the system and he/she is consistently in the office, then a software system might work for you. For multiple users, who work both in and out of the office, consider using a Web-based system.

2. Does the system have a contact manager or just an email auto response system?

If you already have a contact management program, you may only need an email auto responder. If you are not currently using a contact management program, then switch to one with both contact management and email automatic response features.

3. Will the system integrate with my existing traditional CRM system?

If your existing CRM program has open source coding, then most email marketing database programs will easily integrate with your current program.

4. Does your system track email open rates, bounce-backs, and/or click-through rates? If no, can you build that functionality?

Most CRM systems have this feature, but check with the CRM company before purchasing.

5. Does the system flag and/or eliminate duplicates?

This is a critical feature to keep your database clean and efficient. Do not buy any program that does not perform this function.

6. Does the system automate email follow-up? Can I set the follow-up schedule?

This is another critical feature if you receive more than twenty-five online leads per week. Don't buy a system that doesn't automate your follow-up schedule for you.

7. Are system upgrades automatically rolled out to current subscribers? Is there a fee?

Subscribers should automatically receive updates without a fee.

8. Is there a one-time set-up fee for using the system?

Advanced CRM systems require a flat fee to integrate with your traditional CRM system. Expect to pay a couple thousand dollars for set-up.

9. Does the system automatically remove customers who ask to be removed? If no, can you build this functionality?

Most CRM systems will automatically perform this function.

10. How quickly are online leads funneled into the system from my website and other referral websites?

Most CRM systems funnel online leads instantly.

11. Does the CRM system automatically set up reminder to-do tasks?

Mid-size to large home builders or companies who receive a high volume of online leads, should buy a system that automatically sets up to-do and follow-up tasks.

12. Does the CRM system integrate with Outlook?

Most OSCs want to receive a notification in their email software (such as Outlook) whenever they receive an online lead. They also want to be able to email from Outlook and have those emails automatically stored within the CRM.

Create a Follow-Up Plan and Schedule

Good online lead programs have a well-crafted work flow process to follow-up on leads and convert them to an onsite appointment. The length and intensity of the follow-up process is determined by the type of product sold, the characteristics of your target market, and local market conditions.

Good Follow-up Plans Define the Following:

1. Goal—What action do you want the online lead to take?

2. Type—What contact method (phone, email, mail)?

3. Timing—When will the follow-up be delivered?

4. Responsibility—Who will deliver the follow-up?

Sample Follow-Up Schedule

Follow-up Type	Timing
1. Auto-response from website	1. Instant
2. Phone call and personalized email	2. Within minutes
3. Mail follow-up	3. Same day
4. Email follow-up #3	4. Day 7
5. Email follow-up #4 and phone call	5. Day 14
6. Email follow-up #5	6. Day 21
7. Email follow-up #6	7. Day 28
8. Ongoing eNewsletter	8. Forever!

In the sample schedule above, all of the automatic response emails are delivered within twenty-eight days. You may want to vary the time frame of your follow-up based on your target audience. Don't wait too long on the initial follow-up. You don't want the prospect forgetting who you are and deleting the emails because he/she thought you were a spammer.

After you define your follow-up plans, the final step is to load the schedule and email auto-response letters into your CRM system. The follow-up plan continues until the online lead responds, agrees to an appointment, or asks to be removed from your email list.

Ten Most Common Email Follow-Up Mistakes and How to Avoid Them

1. The FROM email address is not specific, is unprofessional, and/or resembles SPAM.

Do you open email from people you don't know? NO. With computer viruses running rampant, consumers are increasingly skeptical about email they receive from unknown sources. Even though you are responding to their request, if the person doesn't recognize your email address, they will delete the email without opening it. Sales people using personal email addresses, such as buffy212@yahoo.com and hotpants911@msn.com, are deleted from their prospect's email inbox or collected in their spam filter. Personal email addresses diminish your credibility and professionalism. Your FROM email address should use your name and company name. This demonstrates the sender is a trusted source and not a spammer.

2. The SUBJECT line of the email is not specific, is unprofessional, and/or sounds like SPAM.

Emails live or die by the subject line. It is the number one determining factor in email open rates. If your subject line is generic, cliché, or sounds like SPAM (meaning it sounds too good to be true), you will be blocked by SPAM filters. Never use $$$, FREE, or Urgent in the subject line. Those are red flags to spam filters.

Remember that many email programs, like Outlook, don't show the entire subject line. Be brief so the majority of the subject line will show in the recipient's inbox. EmailLabs.com has a terrific FROM & SUBECT line tool, which allows you to see exactly how your emails will appear in various email programs such as AOL, Yahoo, Hotmail, Outlook, and many more.

3. The content of the email is poorly written with grammar and spelling mistakes.

Each email must be professionally written. Spelling errors and poor grammar are not acceptable. Mistakes reflect the credibility of your company. Run spell check and proof everything before you send it. While your email should be conversational, it should always have proper spelling and grammar.

4. The email is too long.

Customers don't read email, they scan for sound bites. If your email is too long, your customer will delete it. Email copy must follow the rule of KISS—Keep It Simple Stupid.

5. The email content is too generic and sounds like a form letter.

Would you call a potential buyer and read them a form letter? No, of course not. Then why are you sending generic emails? Your email communication must be as unique as your product. It must demonstrate why someone should buy from you and why you are the best option for your prospect.

6. The email does not have contact information.

Many home builders fail to include their complete contact information in their emails. Providing full contact information demonstrates that you are a legitimate business and not a spammer.

To comply with the CAN SPAM Act,[18] you must include a physical address on every commercial bulk email. Simply include your address in your email signature and it is then automatically included on every email you send out. To create a signature in Outlook, go to the Tools Menu and choose Options. In the Options Menu, choose the Mail Format tab. At the bottom of the Mail Format tab, click on Signatures. Click on the Edit option and you can type a default signature for every email.

7. The email does not contain a call to action or incentive.

Very few emails give a reason to continue the dialogue. Creating urgency about your one-of-a-kind product is a basic sales concept that applies to both your email and traditional marketing media. You have to give people a reason to do business with you. What is your defining feature or benefit? What does the consumer need to know about you that separates you from everyone else? Make that factor clear in every email you send out. Your emails must call the consumer to action because the VALUE you offer is overwhelming.

8. The email is incorrectly formatted.

How the email looks after you finish writing it and how it looks to the recipient can vary, depending on the email program your prospect uses. I receive many responses that are hard to read because of font size, color, and type. Some responses have whole paragraphs that look like Egyptian hieroglyphics. Have you tested your email to see what it looks like after passing through various email browsers? You may be surprised. Most email marketing database programs automatically format emails for you. Create an email template for yourself with the proper spacing and save it as a draft in your email browser.

9. The email is boring.

Photographs and videos are very popular on the Web. Using text email is okay, but you need to provide links in the email to your website photo gallery and virtual tours. You should also include your logo in the header of the email and a photo of the online sales counselor in the email signature.

10. No additional follow-up.

There are many reasons you don't hear back from consumers after you send the first email response. The following are ten reasons why consumers don't respond the first time:

1. The email didn't make it through their spam filter.

2. The message was lost in a packed inbox.

3. Your email was deleted by accident.

4. Someone else using their computer deleted your email.

5. The prospect was too busy to respond.

6. The prospect was on vacation.

7. The prospect is comparing offers.

8. The recipient didn't like your response.

9. Your email was filed for future review.

10. The prospect forgot to respond.

Are you failing to follow up with online leads because you believe they are tire kickers and not serious shoppers? You should always follow up with your online leads regardless of whether you believe they are serious shoppers or not. Remember: never send more than one email per day and preferably no more than one per week.

The Spam Trap and How to Avoid It

Email marketing done right results in sales. Consumers who give you permission to contact them appreciate hearing from you. In fact, they want to hear from you.

Spam is a billion-dollar industry and is so out of control that it threatens the very existence of legitimate email marketing. Every time I open my email inbox, there is some type of offer to enlarge a part of my body (which would be physically impossible), refinance my home, or help me find a date (which I really don't need help with).

Consumers are so sick of unwanted email that they suffer from THD Syndrome—Trigger Happy Deleting. They will delete any and all email that even closely resembles spam.

What does this hypersensitivity mean?

- You must be 100 percent above reproach in how you collect your email addresses.

- You must take proactive measures with your FROM and SUBJECT lines on your email so you are not confused with spam.

- You must comply with the CAN SPAM Act of 2003 or face fines and penalties.

The CAN-SPAM Act

The acronym CAN-SPAM is derived from the bill's full name, Controlling the Assault of Non-Solicited Pornography and Marketing Act.[19] It was signed into law in 2003 to establish the first national standards for sending of commercial email. While it is not widely enforced, the act provides guidelines for businesses to follow about the best practices in email marketing. For a complete understanding and interpretation of this law, you should consult your attorney. This summary is provided for general information only and should not be used in place of legal counsel. Even if your company sends out only permission-based email, the CAN SPAM Act may require you to change the way you send email.

For commercial electronic messages meant to promote a product, service, or content on a website operated for commercial purposes, here is an email checklist:

- Do you have a valid FROM email address?

- Is the SUBJECT line misleading?

- Is the FROM email address a working email and available for at least thirty days?

- Is a physical postal address included in the email message?

- Is your domain name registration (your www address) accurate?

- Did you gather your email list appropriately with opt-in, permission-based methods?

- Does the email make sense to a potential recipient?

- Is the message relevant to the target audience?

- Is your Privacy Policy posted on your website? Does every email link to your Privacy Policy?

Additional Suggestions to Avoid the Spam Trap

1. NEVER add someone to your email distribution list without written permission.

The best kind of permission is called Opt-In permission. This means the user used their mouse to check a box on your website and indicate a desire to receive information from you. Most businesses use registration forms on their website, but most forms do not include an opt-in check box. Permission to email the person is assumed because he/she completed the online registration form. Maybe the person completing the form doesn't want an email; maybe he/she would prefer a phone call or direct mail. Completing the online form isn't enough. I strongly encourage you to add an opt-in check box to your registration form requiring permission to send out e-updates.

2. Don't convert your existing database of consumers and other business partners into an email database.

Just because you already have a mailing database does not give you permission to bulk email those customers. Send one email to the list and ask customers to check the opt-in box on your website to receive email updates from you. Only send email to the people who opt-in.

The same logic applies to your business partners and vendors. Exchanging business cards at a networking function doesn't give you the liberty to add that person to your newsletter list. You must receive permission first.

3. Periodically re-qualify your email database.

It is a waste of time and money to send emails to people who are no longer in the market for your product. Send a short email survey to your entire database every six months and ask if customers are still in the market and, if not, why they did not buy from you. This information is invaluable.

You can dramatically increase your conversion rate of online leads to sales if you have a dedicated person, CRM system, and follow-up process. It will take six to nine months to develop a pipeline of leads and nurture them into sales. However, once the program takes off, the sales curve rapidly builds.

CHAPTER 6

Your Click Power strategy is almost complete. Building Block #4 is critical: closing the sale. **Your online experience and your offline experience must both WOW your customer.** If your online experience is fantastic, but your sales person lacks the WOW factor, then you have let your customer down.

The difference between your online and onsite customer service could make or break your sale. Think about the car dealership example again. What if you had a GREAT experience with the online salesperson, but when you arrived at the dealership nothing was as promised? You would be angry, disillusioned, and probably not purchase a car from that dealership.

- How well do your new home sales counselors present, demonstrate, and close online shoppers?

- Do they take online appointments seriously? Do they understand the VALUE of an online prospect who takes the time to visit a retail location?

It is very difficult to entice an online shopper out of their desk chair. However, when the prospect does visit or agrees to an appointment, you must take that as a VERY positive buying signal. Online shoppers are more likely to buy than traditional walk-in traffic. Why? Because they've done extensive homework online before they walk into your office. On-line shoppers know as much about your product as you do. They know as much about your competition as you do. They know your product's specifications, price, and, often, its limitations. They show up anyway and they want to buy.

The first step is for new home salespeople to ask, "Have you vis-ited our website?"

The National Association of Realtors 2013 Digital House Hunt report found that 90 percent used the Internet to shop for new homes, and real estate related searches have grown 253 percent over the past four years.[20] Most shoppers today have visited your website and your competition's website.

Follow-up with, "What did you see that you liked?"

The answer to this next question provides tremendous insight into the buying motivation of the prospect and gives you a foundation to build upon. Once you learn what brought the shopper to your office or model, or why they are interested in your product or service, you can work to-ward closing the sale.

None of the previous building blocks matter if your sales team isn't ready, willing, and able to close the sale. We focus so much time on finding ready, willing, and able prospects, but often forget to make sure our sales professionals possess the same qualities. Train, coach, and evaluate your sales team regularly to ensure they are high quality, relationship-oriented closers.

This section of *Click Power* is dedicated to all the master new home sales professionals I've had the pleasure to train and coach. You are wonderful. If you are a business owner, I highly encourage you to make this book, particularly this section, required reading for your sales people.

Think Like the Easy Button

My philosophy on how to achieve success in new home sales is best explained in the following quote by Jeffrey Gitomer. "People don't like to be sold, but they love to buy."[21] That is a subtle, yet important difference. Helping people buy a home is about making it easy to buy. This requires a PROACTIVE sales approach. Proactive salespeople actively work at all aspects of the sales process from greeting to closing. They genuinely care about people and want to find the home that fits the buyer's lifestyle best. They are energetic and enthusiastic, even on days they would rather stay in bed.

On a scale of one to ten, how proactive are you?

Are you in the game working for every sale, or sitting back waiting for sales to come to you?

Think of yourself as the easy button of new home sales. You remove obstacles for the buyer, either real or imagined. You educate, counsel, and problem-solve until a path toward homeownership becomes clear.

Proactive new home salespeople take their job seriously and see themselves as sales professionals and not order takers. Proactive salespeople are willing to work diligently and constantly upgrade their skills. They want to be the best in the industry and see sales as a career, not just a job.

An important aspect of staying proactive is earning professional designations such as CSP (Certified New Home Sales Professional), Master CSP, and MIRM (Master of the Institute of Residential Marketing). I highly encourage you to invest your time and money in these valuable education courses. To learn more about available designations go to nahb.org.

The New "E" Meet and Greet

More than any other step, the meet and greet impacts the online customer the most. Before the Internet, meet and greets happened in person. Today it happens digitally.

What kind of first impression does your builder or community make on the Web? Does your Web presence inspire confidence and credibility? Does your website offer a personalized meet and greet, compelling visitors to take the next step and visit you in person?

Website visitors look for many reasons to eliminate you during their search process. One reason they eliminate you is because of an unprofessional website that is hard to navigate. Generally, most prospective buyers select three to five neighborhoods to investigate further.

If you make the cut, prospective buyers will take one of several actions:

- Register online or email the agent for more information.

- Call the community.

- Visit the community in person.

- Nothing.

From my experience reviewing home builder Google Analytics reports and comparing them to lead capture reports, on average only 1 – 2 percent of your website traffic actually completes the online registration form. The vast majority of your website traffic calls, visits in person, or does nothing.

Make sure your website makes it simple for someone to call or visit. Post your contact information in a highly visible place on the Web page. Don't forget to include detailed driving directions, local area maps, and model center hours as well. I also encourage you to place your picture on the page next to a welcome message to personalize the visitor's web experience.

The New Phone Greeting

With so many of your website visitors calling for more information, it is important to maximize each phone call and set as many appointments as possible. When people call for more information, don't just answer questions and allow them to hang up. Instead, engage them in a conversation that will move the sales cycle along. Use these general tips as a guide, and customize your conversations to your company and product.

1. Answer the phone with a consistent, branded greeting.

Salesperson: "Thanks for calling Birchbend Estates. This is Meredith speaking, and you are?" This greeting clearly identifies the community and salesperson, as well as asking the caller for their name.

2. Never just give out information and then hang up. Ask a question to open a conversation.

Caller: "Oh, hi, this is Allen. What are your model home hours?"

Salesperson: "Nice to meet you, Allen. Our hours are weekdays 11 a.m. to 6 p.m. and weekends noon to 5 p.m. When do you plan on stopping by?"

Caller: "Sometime this weekend. I don't really know yet."

Salesperson: "Okay. I'm just curious, Allen, how did you hear about our community?" OR "Great. I'm just curious, have you visited our website?"

Caller: "Yes, I visited the website and that's how I found you."

Salesperson: "Great. Which one of our floor plans did you like the best?"

Caller: "I don't remember the name, but I like a couple of the two-story plans."

3. Give the caller a reason to visit and a reason to make an appointment.

Salesperson: "Allen, our master on the main two-story plan is very popular. You know, I have one of those under construction you could take a look at when you stop by. When can I schedule an appointment for you?"

Caller: "Well, I guess this weekend."

Salesperson: "This weekend is perfect. We only have a few home sites still available for a two-story floor plan. We are very busy on the weekends. What time should we make an appointment, so I can reserve time to show you our home site and answer any questions you may have? Would Saturday or Sunday work better for you? What time works best?"

Caller: "I could come on Sunday after church around 1 p.m."

4. Ask for a phone number so you can confirm the appointment twenty-four hours in advance.

Salesperson: "Terrific, Allen. Let me give you my direct phone number, just in case something comes up. What is your number? Do you need directions? Is there anything else I can prepare for your visit? I can't wait to meet you."

The New In-Person Greeting

"Have you visited our website" is not just a question for callers anymore. Begin asking everyone who walks in without an appointment if they visited your website. Ask walk-ins:

- Have you visited our website?

- Which of our floor plans did you select?

- What interests you about our community?

- Did you try our mortgage calculator?

- What other builder or neighborhood websites did you visit? See anything you liked?

The website question is a natural conversation starter. It also gives your sales presentation a clear path once you know what the prospect liked most about your company enough to visit in person. Replace your canned sales presentation with the website question. Unless asked, most prospects won't admit that they've visited the website or printed out information. However, when you ask, most will share their likes, dislikes, and even pull the printed pages out of their purse or pocket.

By establishing early-on that the prospect visited your website, used the mortgage calculator, and selected a favorite floor plan, you have qualified that buyer. This is an immediate B-Back. WOW. Do the happy dance because you are about to make a sale.

The New Qualify

Even though the online customer is a B-Back on their very first visit, you will still need to ask a few qualifying questions:

- Who will live in the home?

- What is most important to you?

- Where do you work?

- Where do you live now?

- When do you want to move into your new home?

- Why move now?

Don't forget to ask the most important qualifying question: Why do you want to buy a new home?

 The *why* question reveals the buyer's motivation for shopping with you. When you understand motivation, you understand how to help them buy.

I once bought a new home because of my dog, Molly Oliver, and an old truck. We were living in a neighborhood that was hit hard by Hurricane Charley. The neighborhood never really recovered and eventually declined. My next-door neighbor rented to a couple of tenants who decided to park their rusty, red pickup truck in front of our house.

My office was located in the front bedroom and had a lovely bay window. Molly sat on my desk every day and looked out the window. It was her window to the world. With the rusty, red pickup parked there, Molly's view was obstructed. That would never do. So we went shopping for a home that allowed Molly the view she deserves.

The point of the story is that without asking me the *why* question, you would never know what was really motivating me. Scary as that answer is, it's the truth. A salesperson who understood my home buying motivations could have helped me buy a lovely view for Molly Oliver.

In my seminars I teach salespeople to think like Curious George. When it comes to qualifying, you can't ask too many questions. I promise you aren't asking enough. Start being more aware of your ratio of information received, to questions asked. Remember: inquiring minds want to know.

The key to asking questions—lots of questions—is your delivery. If you come across like Tony Soprano shining the light in someone's eyes with the threat of broken kneecaps, then your questions are not well-received. However, if you come across like a knowledgeable, friendly advisor who wants to find the best solution for your customer, then your questions are welcome.

Presenting and demonstrating is easy when you've done a good job qualifying. When an online customer visits a community, he/she wants the real story and not the sales pitch on the builder's website. The customers want the real, inside information only PROFESSIONALS know.

Online customers expect to speak to an expert who possesses:

- In-depth product knowledge.

- Complete understanding of the construction process.

- Thorough knowledge of brand partners' products.

- Detailed information on schools, entertainment, shopping, and local area attractions.

- Insight on flexible financing options beyond the thirty-year fixed.

- Current market information on average sales prices and interest rates.

When presenting to customers, teach them information they can't find online. If you sound like a talking version of the website, feature-dumping the pricing, amenities, and floor plan options, the customer will walk away. Why bother visiting?

Online customers look for a trusted advisor who can help them buy a home. To do that, you need to ask lots of questions about how they plan to use the home, and then use your knowledge and experience to pair them with the right home.

I recently bought new family-room furniture. I am normally very decisive, but this decision was dragging on forever. I visited many furniture stores and still could not find exactly what I was looking for. Then I met April. She worked for a national furniture chain, and from the moment I walked into the store, she WOWED me. Every other sales person asked one to two routine questions and then brought me furniture samples and began describing the furniture.

April looked at me inquisitively and asked me questions like:

- Do you entertain in this room?

- Do you watch TV in this room? How often? What are your favorite TV shows?

- Do you have pets? Kids? (That's when I broke out the pictures.)

- Do you like to sit or lie down to watch TV?

- Do you like your feet up?

- Would you prefer fabric or leather? Would you say your style is more traditional or contemporary?

- Would you prefer a sofa and loveseat combination or a sofa and over-stuffed chair with ottoman combination?

She did all this in such a caring manner that the volume of the questions didn't bother me at all. In fact, it had the opposite effect. I felt like April was on my team. She was such a great sales person that I tried to recruit her for new home sales.

A website doesn't offer what April offers. She offers experience and knowledge. She is exactly what the online customer wants. April helped clarify my thinking, which enabled me to make a decision. She also clearly followed a sales process. Once she finished presenting and demonstrating, she closed me with a "timing close" (I could have the furniture by Christmas if I ordered that day).

What if April had just pointed out the various family room furniture collections and their prices? I already knew that information from the company's website. I visited the store in person because I knew the style of the furniture was a match for my style. However, I didn't have a CLUE about which collection would suit my lifestyle best.

Online customers preselect your company based on the overall look and feel of your homes and community from your website. However, they might not always KNOW what will work best for them. The proactive sales person thinks like Curious George and asks questions to find out what will fit the family best. This approach truly is about helping people buy.

The second most important aspect of presenting to online customers is helping them experience the product with interactive demonstrations. Best Buy and Brookstone know that when **PEOPLE PLAY, PEOPLE PAY**. When you visit either store, plenty of samples are available for play. How many husbands spend most of their time at the mall in a Brookstone massage chair? How many do you think Brookstone sold as a result? Tons. (It worked on mine.)

Get out of your desk chair and into the model homes, inventory homes, under-construction homes, and recently-built homes. If you don't have any sample product to show, then break out the blueprints and demonstrate from paper. The faster you can encourage online customers to interact with your product, the sooner you will close more sales. Car dealers understand this. When you look at new cars, you don't spend a lot of time in the sales office. You go straight onto the lot and start test-driving models.

I believe customers relax and open up when you walk and talk at the same time. Once you qualify the customer and have an understanding of what they need, go to the product as quickly as possible. The goal should always be to demonstrate the three key areas that are most important to the customer, whether that is the master bedroom/bath, family room, and bonus room, or the home's exterior, home office, and kitchen.

As you demonstrate each area, continue to ask questions about how the customer would use the space. Relate your detailed product knowledge to their needs. This is a great opportunity to share information about your brand partners (i.e. Moen faucets, Whirlpool appliances, and Mohawk flooring). As you discover what would fit the family's lifestyle, trial close with questions like: "Can you see yourself cooking in this kitchen?" or "Would this family room suit you?"

However, use caution. Only demonstrate sample products that match the customer's needs. Don't walk them through your one and only model because that's all you have available. Find product that is closest to what the customer is looking for, whether it's inventory or under construction, and start with those samples. You can always finish the demonstration with a walk-through of the model home for the customer to see the quality and options available. Nothing is more irritating to the customer than wasting time looking at things that don't remotely match their interests.

Establishing One-of-a-Kind

Don't forget to demonstrate the DIRT. The most underutilized sales tools are home sites. The location or *dirt* in your community is the truest one-of-a-kind product you have. Your competitors probably have similar floor plans to yours, but the home sites and their characteristics only exist in one place at one time. Your home sites are limited and available to only a select few. By focusing on the type of home site your prospect wants, you narrow down the possible choices and create a sense of urgency.

Home site information cannot be accurately described online. It takes an in-person visit to really appreciate the view, orientation, and size of a home site. Are you asking every prospect about the kind of home site he/she would prefer? Remember to think like Curious George and ask these questions:

- What do you like about your current home site?

- What would you change about it?

- What exposure (north, south, east, or west) do you prefer?

- Is view important to you? If so, what type of view do you prefer?

- Do you entertain outdoors? Play sports? Have animals that need room to play?

- Do you envision needing or wanting a pool or playground in the future?

After asking these questions, you are ready to take your prospects to look at homes and home sites. You have helped them narrow down their choices so they can interact with the product.

Remember, when people play, people pay. It's that simple.

The New Follow-Up

You might have noticed I didn't include a separate section for closing. I don't believe closing needs its own chapter. **I believe closing is a PROCESS and not a one-time event.** Closing a sale occurs when a new home salesperson follows the steps I've previously outlined. However, when it doesn't, that's where your follow-up makes the difference.

I am not saying you don't have to ask for the sale. You do. You have to ask your prospects, "Is this your house?" But what I *am* saying is that asking the closing question is much easier when you've followed a proven sales process.

You can only ask closing questions when buying signals are present. **If someone isn't sure, needs more time, or needs to confer with another stakeholder, then follow-up is your best friend.** Vary your methods to include email, phone calls, and handwritten mail. All forms of follow-up are important and serve a purpose. It is important to match the communication style to the prospect's preferred style. In this section, I am going to focus on email follow-up, but that isn't meant to imply that other methods are less important or powerful.

Consumers receive so much email that they limit the number of *relationships* to a select few. Think about your own inbox. You probably pay more attention to transactional email, such as order confirmations and bank account information. Travel, hobby, and news-related emails are also viewed as important. With the amount of email we pay attention to, it doesn't leave much room for your follow-up messages. **Make each email to customers relevant, compelling, and unique.**

Remember: online leads and/or walk-in traffic asked for information and want to hear from you. You are not spamming them with follow-up email. You are a professional who earned the right to contact them by giving them precious time during the first visit. However, if your messages are bland and generic, your prospect will hit the delete button every time.

Use these follow-up tips when writing your emails:

1. **Inject personality into your email.** Don't open with the standard first line, "Thank you for stopping by" or "It was a pleasure to meet you," which sounds like a generic form letter. This greeting doesn't sound personal or interesting. Use a greeting like "Hi again, how is the home shopping going?" Reintroduce yourself just like you would if you were seeing them again in person. **The communications and rapport skills that work in the offline world work very well in the online world.**

I know most salespeople are not professional copywriters. I am not asking you to write perfect prose. Your gift is your ability to connect with people, establishing rapport, asking questions, and ultimately helping them find exactly what they want and need. Use the skills that work so well for you in the offline world, in your writing in the online world. Let's be honest; with the overwhelming amount of digital communication than occurs today, the ability to write clear, concise, and compelling copy has become a necessary skill for all salespeople. If writing is not your strongest skill, consider taking a writing course or hiring an assistant to help you.

Today's consumer requires a new breed of salesperson that connects both in person and digitally. Think of your email as an electronic handshake reaching out and welcoming people to your community. You want prospects to view you as friendly, responsive, warm, and the ultimate authority on new homes in your market. You know everyone and everyone knows you. You are a resource. You know more about the competition than your buyers. You have copies of articles for buyers to read and websites they can research for more information. You are the ultimate information broker who closes the sale because people know you care about them.

2. **Write like you talk.** Write the email as if the person was standing in front of you in the model center. What would you normally say?

What key phrases and points do you want to make sure they understand about your builder and neighborhood? What questions do you ask to tailor your presentation? You can do the same with your email messages. The only caveat is making sure your email is grammatically correct and doesn't contain slang words. Always run spell check and have someone else proofread your messages.

3. Be creative. Don't simply write the same old boring copy you've read everywhere else. Help your neighborhood and your builder stand out among the deluge of other emails consumers receive. Sound more like you are offering a personal service rather than a form letter acknowledging receipt of their request.

4. Use technology to stand out. Snap a few photos of the home they liked and create a collage with an app like Pic Stitch. You can email or post it to social media with the click of one button. Or shoot a 360-degree panoramic video of their favorite home site or community amenity with an app like 360Panorama.

5. Do the opposite of everyone else. If everyone else is sending text messages and email follow-up, blow your prospects away with handwritten notes or a personalized postcard featuring a photo of their favorite home exterior. Apps like Postagram, justWink, ink, and Cardstore allow you to create stunning, full-color personalized cards that the app mails for you. For a couple of dollars per card you can knock your prospects socks off.

Go back through Chapter 5, Building Block #3, and review the tips I gave Online Sales Counselors on how to follow up with Internet leads. Many of those same strategies work very well for onsite sales counselors who are working with walk-in traffic.

CHAPTER 7

If you implemented the first four building blocks, you now have a very functional online sales and marketing strategy. Online shoppers are finding your website in search engines, your website is wowing visitors, and your follow-up process is nurturing online leads to sales. Awesome. The last step is to measure your program's success and track your long-term goals.

Review the following analytics reports monthly:

- Social media

- Email marketing

- SEO

- Paid search

- CRM

- Website

Social Media Analytics

If you are marketing on a Facebook business page, the Insights Report is invaluable because it gives you feedback on how well users are engaging with your content. The Posts Report lists each post and gives the reach and engagement numbers. Reach is defined as the number of people your post was served to. The higher the reach number, the more people saw the post. This is helpful because you will notice trends in terms of posting day and time that influence the reach number. By analyzing the optimal time to reach your audience, you can make sure the largest possible number sees your content.

Engagement is measured by the post clicks, comments, likes, or shares a post receives. Photos, graphics, and videos always have the highest numbers. By studying what engages your audience, you can tailor your content to their interests and reach even higher levels. This is important not only for your marketing and sales goals, but the more engaging your posts, the higher Facebook will rank them in the Newsfeed algorithm. The higher your posts show in the Newsfeed and the longer they stay there, the more engagement and visibility your posts receive.

The Facebook Insights Reports also offer valuable information about the demographics and geographic locations of your followers. Review this information and make sure your Facebook followers are a reflection of your target audience. If they are not, consider running some paid ads to reach out to users more in line with your audience.

One last area to monitor on the Facebook Insights Report is the New Likes and Unlikes. Watch for spikes or dips in these numbers, and then see if that activity correlates to content that was posted. Perhaps you hosted an Open House luncheon for a group of real estate agents, and the number of page likes spiked that day. Now you know that type of event is a good way to market your Facebook page. Or conversely, you may have over-posted one month and irritated your followers. Perhaps your content wasn't appealing or, even worse, offensive in some way and caused the number of unlikes to spike. Most pages will have a steady number of unlikes each month. The key is to avoid spikes that could have been avoided.

If you're looking for more in-depth social media reporting, I like the

Sprout Social platform. For $59/month, you can monitor, publish, and report on up to ten social media profiles (this only includes one user login). The Facebook and Twitter reports in Sprout are easy to generate and interpret. Sprout also offers Engagement Reports that rank your engagement level, and Competition Reports where you can compare two profiles against each other.

Other third-party social media dashboard platforms that you can look at include Hootsuite and Tweetdeck. Hootsuite is much more affordable in terms of day-to-day management monitoring and publishing ($9.99/month), but the reports included in that fee are rather basic. You can order more advanced reports, but they cost extra. I haven't used Tweetdeck so I can't give you a personal review on it.

Email Marketing Reports

I love reviewing email marketing reports. I know it sounds geeky, but there is so much you can learn from them.

Key stats to watch:

- **Total Delivered** – This is the total number of emails successfully delivered.

- **Open Rate** – This is the percentage of subscribers who opened the email from the number successfully delivered.

- **Click-Through Rate** – This is the percentage of subscribers who clicked on at least one link in the email from the number successfully delivered.

- **Bounce Rate** – This is the percentage of undeliverable emails.

- **Opens** – This report shows you which subscribers opened the email and how many times they have opened it.

- **Clicks** – This report shows you who clicked on what links and how many times they have clicked.

- **Unsubscribes** – This is the total number of subscribers who asked to be removed from the email list.

- **Abuse Reports** – The number of recipients who reported your email as spam to their email provider.

Search Engine Optimization (SEO)

Do not measure the effectiveness of your search engine marketing efforts by Googling your desired keywords. Why? First, Google personalizes the search results to the user based on past browsing history and geographic location. What you see in the search results and what someone else sees can be completely different. Have you ever noticed that the paid Google search ads will display results for your geographic location even though you are purposely looking for a business/service in a different location? Google knows where you are.

Second, search engine rankings are not the only measure of effectiveness. A more effective measurement is the amount of Google Organic Traffic coming to your website. A website that has been properly optimized will see an increase in Google Organic Traffic. Allow at least six months for a SEO campaign to show results, and remember search volume varies seasonally. Typically, home builder Google Organic search traffic drops in November, December, July, and August; so if traffic is down one month, don't assume the SEO campaign isn't working. It's best to compare Google Organic Traffic numbers year over year versus month over month to account for any seasonal changes.

Your SEO vendor should proactively provide monthly rankings and analytics reports, and offer insight on how to interpret them. At Creating WOW, we hold monthly SEO calls for every client and review all of the numbers at that time. We brainstorm new marketing ideas and talk about how to improve the SEO effectiveness.

Paid Search Marketing

Google Adwords offers a lot of great reporting options. At a minimum, look at the Campaign Summary report at the top of the Home screen. This report shows you the number of clicks, impressions, average cost per click, and total spend amount for the date range compared to the previous thirty days. It is an easy way to see month over month how your campaign is performing at a very high level.

If you want even more information, review the Keyword report, which shows you how many clicks, impressions, average cost per click, and total spend per keyword phrases. This report is incredibly helpful to refine your campaign because you can see which phrases are producing the most clicks and how much those clicks cost. If a phrase is producing a lot of clicks, but also eating up the majority of the budget to the exclusion of other needed phrases, you may want to lower the bid amount on that phrase. This report also shows you underperforming phrases that are not driving traffic due to low search volume or low quality score.

Another place to monitor Google Adwords is within Google Analytics for your website. The two accounts are not automatically connected, so your first step is to connect them. Go to Account Settings>Linked Accounts>Google Analytics in your Google Adwords account, and that is where you can link the two together. Once they are linked, you will be able to see Google CPC (cost per click) as a traffic source in the Google Analytics/Acquisition/All Traffic Report. The benefit to this is you can see the average time on site, average number of pages viewed, bounce rate, and goal conversions of the PPC campaign. As we discussed earlier, these numbers are very important to assessing the quality of a traffic source.

The benefit of using a vendor partner to manage your paid search marketing is that they can monitor the campaign performance for you and summarize the results in a once-a-month report. The biggest mistake most builders make with paid search marketing is trying to manage it in-house and then getting too busy to properly monitor it. Refining the campaign, tweaking keywords, ad copy, bid amounts, and budgets are all KEY to driving more leads with paid search marketing.

CRM Reports

Which CRM reports are important to review depends **greatly** on which CRM software you use. Because I don't know what reports your software offers, it's hard for me to be too specific on this topic, but here are a few guidelines to show what you should be monitoring through CRM.

- **Total Traffic by Community** – Total traffic by community allows you to compare which communities are receiving the most traffic and measures the effectiveness of campaigns promoting specific communities.

- **Online Leads** – The number of leads generated by your website or social media profiles. Includes emails, phone calls from the website, live chats, and social media inquiries.

- **Traffic by Lead Sources** – The number of leads (both online and in-person) generated by traffic source as reported by your sales agents.

- **Salesperson Activity** – Breakdown on the follow-up activities of the sales people to include phone calls, emails, first appointments, second appointments, online chats, etc.

- **Sales Conversion** – Percentage by sales agent of leads to sales. This would indicate how well a sales person is converting traffic.

- **Pipeline Summary** – Snapshot of the number of leads in the pipeline in various stages of shopping.

Website

The most important website* statistics are:

*These definitions are based on the definitions provided by Google Analytics. If you are not using Google Analytics, please consult the glossary of terms for your analytics program before extrapolating these definitions to your own data.

1. **Sessions**—This number represents the total number of visits to a website during a specified period of time. How do you know if your number is above, below, or even with the average for your market? Look at your overall marketing. How often do you market the web-site online? How often do you use offline media, including print, signage, and/or broadcast media? The more you market, the more visits to your website should increase. If you do not see a positive correlation to marketing and website visits, rethink your market-ing component mix. As you browse monthly numbers, remember to think less about where you are right now, and more about how your numbers grow as you implement the Wagon Wheel method of driving traffic to your website.

2. **Users**—This number represents the number of visitors to the website (both new and returning) within the date range. The ratio of sessions to users is a good indicator of how many visitors are returning to your website. You want a healthy balance of first-time visitors and returning visitors.

3. **Pages/Visit**—This number represents the average number of pages viewed by a visitor during one session. On average, most visitors will view one to two pages per minute. The larger your website, the more pages that should be viewed each session. Think about your own browsing habits. How long do you stay and how many pages do you view when you don't like a website?

4. **Average Time on Site**—This number represents the average visit

length for visitors. A good benchmark for home builders is three to five minutes, depending on the size and complexity of your website. If your website routinely keeps visitors attention for five minutes or more, you have a *sticky* website. Remember, content and interactive features help create a sticky website.

5. **Bounce Rate**—This number represents the percentage of single-page visits or visits in which the visitor looked at one page on the website and then left. A benchmark for the Bounce Rate is between 20 – 30 percent. A low Bounce Rate means you aren't marketing your site widely enough because only the low-hanging fruit are visiting the site—visitors that already know your name through a referral. A healthy Bounce Rate means you are reaching a wider audience that may not have heard of your company before. If your rate is too high, it indicates your online marketing is not targeted enough, and the wrong visitors are viewing your website.

6. **% New Visits**—This number represents the percentage of first-time visitors to your website of your total Visits. This number is important because it should increase as your online marketing increases. On home builder websites, I look for a healthy balance (50/50 or 60/40) of Return Visitors and New Visitors, because we know most buyers don't buy after their first visit to a website.

Not only can analytics provide you with important feedback on the overall health of your website, it can provide insight into how visitors found your website and their browsing habits.

Make sure you review the **Traffic Sources** report in Google Analytics. This report lists your top website traffic sources and categorizes them into either Direct Traffic (the visitor typed in your web address, had you saved as a favorite, or clicked on a link in an email), Referring Site Traffic (a visitor clicked through from another website other than a search engine), and Search Engine Traffic (a visitor clicked through to your website from a search engine).

The percentage of visitors in these three areas should correlate to the advertising dollars you spend in each one. Compare the Page Views, Time on Site, % New Visits, Bounce Rate, and Exit Rate with the traffic sources to determine the quality of the traffic per source. Some traffic sources may not deliver the largest quantity of visitors, but the quality is well worth the investment.

The **Top Content** report is important to monitor what information visitors gravitate toward on your website. This information will help you know which pages are most important to update and maintain. Top content reports will also help you prioritize your content and make sure the most important information is highly visible. In my experience reviewing home builder Google Analytics reports, the Community Map Page, Available Homes Page, Photo Gallery, and Videos are the most frequently visited pages. This report will also help you identify if a page is under-performing. If a page has a low average visit length and/or high bounce rate, then the content on the page is not engaging your visitors.

The **Mobile Devices** report tells you how many visits to the website were from mobile devices. This information is invaluable because you can quantify the quality of visits per device and tweak your website accordingly.

Finally, I recommend reviewing the **Conversions** report on a regular basis. This report requires custom set-up by your webmaster. Once set-up, the report tracks the total number of conversions (as defined by you) during a specified time period and what traffic source delivered that conversion. A conversion is defined in a number of ways. The most common way is the number of visitors who complete a Contact Us or Request for Information lead capture form. This report is very powerful since it allows you to not only track the number of leads received, but also what traffic source delivered those leads.

The beauty of online marketing is found in the constant monitoring and measurement of clicks, pages/visit, bounce rate, average length of visit, and percentage of online lead information requests to review the impact of your marketing dollars.

Tips for Reviewing Website Analytics Data:

- Review at least ninety days of data before drawing any performance conclusions.

- Refer to your analytic provider's glossary of terms to interpret the report. For example, not all analytic providers define a *visitor* the same way.

- Set up automated reports to your email once a month to remind you to review the reports regularly.

- Question the data. Look for potential technical or functional problems that you may have overlooked previously.

- If you are new to analytics, consult a Web marketing expert to help you interpret the data so you don't arrive at erroneous conclusions.

- Remember to account for seasonal adjustments in traffic and compare year-to-year numbers for a more accurate analysis.

Online Lead to Sales Conversion Rates

How do you measure the performance of your Online Sales Counselor? After coaching and training many OSCs throughout the years, I've found the following benchmarks as reasonable performance goals. **Please be aware that a new OSC program takes approximately six to nine months to begin showing consistent results.**

- Your OSC should set appointments with a minimum of 25 percent of your online leads each month to visit a community.

- Of the set online lead appointments, approximately 50+ percent will show up for the appointment. If your OSC consistently confirms all appointments, you can increase the rate to 80+ percent.

- Of the kept appointments, you can expect to write agreements with 30 – 80+ percent of those prospects. Let me say that again. Yes, you can expect to write agreements on 30 – 80+ percent of the kept online lead appointments.

Let's say you average 100 online leads per month (remember these are email requests from customers who have only visited your website and NOT visited a sales office). At a minimum, here are the results you can expect:

- 100   Online leads per month

- 25   Set appointments with 25 percent

- 12.5   Kept appointments average 50 – 80 percent

- 3 – 9   Sales converted, 33 percent or more of the kept appointments

If your existing OSC isn't meeting these numbers, then perhaps they could use some sales training on appointment setting, and/or your sales-people might need training on demonstrating and closing.

You can track these conversion numbers via your CRM system. Plan a monthly performance review meeting with the OSC to review the numbers, troubleshoot any problems, and plan new campaigns. Ideally, this meeting would also include your marketing manager to coordinate the online and offline marketing with the OSC's efforts.

The final step is to track online lead to sales conversions. There is no easy way to do this. Most OSCs have to manually cross-reference their online lead database with the weekly sales report. Why? New home consultants are not 100 percent accurate when they source leads, and Web leads are sometimes sourced improperly. It's best to do this manually and make sure the numbers are accurate.

Conclusion

There you have it. You've just learned the Click Power Strategy. You are now ready to handle Web marketing for your business and align it with your overall sales and marketing process. You have the tools to make your website WOW, to market your website, to drive more traffic, and to measure its effectiveness. You also know how to quickly respond to online leads. You even know why it's important that your offline presence matches your online experience.

With these tools, you are well-positioned to stay ahead of your competition, increase sales, and grow your business in any economy.

How do you become the master of your domain?

1. Review The Click Power Strategy. Which building block(s) need more focus? Use this to identify your goals.

2. Map out your current Wagon Wheel of Marketing and your ideal Wagon Wheel. Select the hub and traffic drivers that make the most sense for your business.

3. What specific action steps are needed to improve your online sales and marketing program?

4. What technology tools do you need to procure or upgrade to be more effective?

5. Identify the knowledge and/or skills you might need, such as additional training, education, coaching, or consulting.

6. Set a deadline for each action step and assign a project leader accountable for that step.

This project is a process and it will take time to work through the stages effectively. Be patient and keep it moving. Don't lose momentum. More leads and more sales are waiting.

Book Meredith Oliver to Speak at Your Next Event

Meredith Oliver is a professional speaker and has given hundreds of presentations to a variety of audiences during the past thirteen years—always to rave reviews.

Meredith delivers:

- Keynote speeches

- In-person sales training seminars

- Web seminar sales training

- Convention/conference break-out sessions

- Banquet hosting and event emcee

- Association programs

- Continuing education programs

- Professional click by click webinars

Visit Creatingwow.com/professional-speaker/ to learn more about Meredith's topics and view a demo video.

"AWESOME JOB! Meredith, you were awesome on Friday. The program went smoothly and we had standing room only. I appreciate all you do and look forward to many years of knowing you and hearing feature seminars."
Cindy Nugent Huber, StructSure Home Warranty

"Meredith is one of the premier professionals in the country regarding Internet marketing in the home building industry. She is an excellent speaker whose presentations are both informative and entertaining. Her expertise on how to 'marry' online and on-site residential marketing provides a blueprint for success for builders, developers, and brokers who want to maximize their investment in their websites, social media, and Internet marketing. I highly recommend Meredith as a speaker and consultant."

Rich Carlson, President, Carlson Communications

"I was at the JAX WCR meeting today and really enjoyed your presentation. You were full of energy, had some great ideas, and had a good sense of humor. I loved the click theme that made it fun for everyone. Good job!"

Christine Baranofsky, Watson Realty Company

Connect With Meredith

CreatingWOW.com

@CreatingWOW

Facebook.com/creatingwow

YouTube.com/mereditholivertv

Linkedin.com/in/mereditholiver

Instagram.com/MeredithsShoes22

The Fan Factor:
25 Slam Dunk Secrets to Engage Customers, Increase Referrals and Boost Sales

The Fan Factor is a social media marketing guidebook on how to engage online fans to increase referrals and sales.

In this age of liking, following, texting, and tweeting, your customers are overwhelmed by an avalanche of marketing messages. Using best practices and case studies, *The Fan Factor* will teach you slam dunk secrets to engage your customers resulting in increased referrals and sales.

Topics Include:

- Generating engagement

- Content marketing

- Blogging best practices

- Social media do's and don'ts

- Technology tools and apps

"Whether you're a social media novice or a seasoned professional, you'll take something away from this book. Meredith's passion for Internet marketing jumps right through the pages and inspires even this hard-to-impress reader. Count me in as the newest member of the Meredith Oliver fan club."
Alex Benshoof, Director of Marketing, Red Door Homes

"The Fan Factor is the perfect combination of resources, information, and real-life practical stories and examples on how to take your social media efforts to the next level."
Leah Turner, Turner Time Consulting, Tampa, FL

"Fan Factor is written as though a good friend was telling you a story, with timely injections of personal anecdotes. It is a quick read, although it took me twice as long to get through because of all the time I spent highlighting passages and bookmarking pages."
Steve McAuliffe, McAuliffe & McCormick Inc.

"Once you can engage your audience, it's much easier to turn them into fans who will buy your products and services, and recommend you to others. That's the premise of the new book, The Fan Factor...This is an excellent book with a ton of useful tips and advice."
Gloria Rand, SEO Copywriter, Blogger

Order today at CreatingWOW.com/FanFactor

End Notes

1 *Study: 81% research online before making big purchases.* Retailing Today, July 12, 2013, http://www.retailingtoday.com/article/study-81-research-online-making-big-purchases.

2 *Internet User Demographics.* Pew Research Internet Project, January 2014 Survey, http://www.pewinternet.org/data-trend/internet-use/latest-stats/.

3 She-conomy.com. Marketing to Women Quick Facts. Statistics. Statistics compiled for the Marketing to Women Conference. http://www.she-conomy.com/report/marketing-to-women-quick-facts.

4 Abraham, Linda Boland; Morn, Marie Pauline; Vollman, Andrea. *Women on the Web: How Women are Shaping the Internet.* comScore Whitepaper. June 30, 2010. http://www.comscore.com/Press_Events/Presentations_Whitepapers/2010/Women_on_the_Web_How_Women_are_Shaping_the_Internet.

5 Redish, Janice. *Letting Go of the Words: Writing Web Content that Works.* San Francisco: Morgan Kaufmann Publishers, 2007.

6 Krug, Steve. *Don't Make Me Think: A Common Sense Approach to Web Usability.* Berkeley: New Riders, 2006.

7 *What Internet Users Do Online.* Trend Data (Adults), Pew Internet & American Life Project, April 2012 survey, http://pewinternet.org/Trend-Data-(Adults)/Online-Activites-Total.aspx.

8 "comScore Releases March 2014 U.S. Search Engine Rankings." comScore, April 2014, https://www.comscore.com/Insights/Press-Releases/2014/4/comScore-Releases-March-2014-U.S.-Search-Engine-Rankings.

9 SearchEngineLand.com. *What is SEO/Search Engine Optimization?* http://searchengineland.com/guide/what-is-seo.

10 Scott, David Meerman. *The New Rules of Marketing and PR: How to Use News Releases, Blogs, Podcasting, Viral Marketing and Online Media to Reach Buyers Directly.* New Jersey: John Wiley & Sons, Inc., 2007.

11 Nielsen Wire. *Consumer Trust in Online, Social and Mobile Advertising Grows.* April 10, 2012. http://blog.nielsen.com/nielsenwire/media_entertainment/consumer-trust-in-online-social-and-mobile-advertising-grows/.

12 David. *How Social Media Influences Consumer Behavior.* Search Engine Marketing Group. July 19, 2010. http://sem-group.net/search-engine-optimization-blog/how-social-media-influences-consumer-behavior/.

13 Oliver, Meredith. *The Fan Factor: 25 Slam Dunk Secrets to Engage Customers, Increase Referrals and Boost Sales.* Self-Published, 2013.

14 Morgan, Carol L. *Social Media 3.0: It's Easier Than You Think.* Washington DC: NAHB BuilderBooks, 2013.

15 Zarella, Dan. *New Data Proves 'Please ReTweet' Generates 4X More Tetweets [Data].* Hubspot Blog. May 31, 2011. http://blog.hubspot.com/blog/tabid/6307/bid/14982/New-Data-Proves-Please-ReTweet-Generates-4x-More-ReTweets-Data.aspx.

16 Oldroyd, James; McElheran, Kristina; Elkington, David. *The Short Life of Online Sales Leads.* Harvard Business Review. March 2011. http://hbr.org/2011/03/the-short-life-of-online-sales-leads/ar/1.

17 *Lead Management Tips.* Powerpoint Presentation. SmartTouch Interactive. May 2013.

18 *CAN-SPAM Act: A Compliance Guide for Business.* Bureau of Consumer Protection Business Center. September 2009. http://business.ftc.gov/documents/bus61-can-spam-act-compliance-guide-business/.

19 CAN-SPAM Act of 2003. Bill Text October 22, 2003. SpamLaws.com. http://www.spamlaws.com/federal/108s877oct22.shtml.

20 *Digital House Hunt.* National Association of Realtors. PDF Download. January 2013. http://www.realtor.org/reports/digital-house-hunt.

21 Gitomer, Jeffrey. *The Patterson Principles of Selling.* John Wiley & Sons, Inc., 2004.

CPSIA information can be obtained at www.ICGtesting.com
Printed in the USA
LVOW01s0706291114

416168LV00002B/2/P